500 RECIPES FOR COOKING FOR ONE

500 RECIPES FOR COOKING FOR ONE

by Catherine Kirkpatrick

HAMLYN

LONDON · NEW YORK · SYDNEY · TORONTO

Contents

Cover photograph by Paul Williams

Published by The Hamlyn Publishing Group Limited
London · New York · Sydney · Toronto
Astronaut House, Feltham, Middlesex, England

© Copyright The Hamlyn Publishing Group Limited 1963

Fifteenth impression 1981

ISBN 0 600 03405 4

Printed and bound in Great Britain by
Morrison & Gibb Ltd., London and Edinburgh

Introduction

If you talk to anyone about cooking you will find that, no matter who it is, he or she has some particular problem connected with their catering. To me the greatest difficulty is that which faces the person who lives alone. Unless you have had to do it yourself you would not believe how difficult it is to shop for small quantities of food. I have often felt envious of the woman in front of me at the checking-out desk in the supermarket—simply because she has a basket crammed with shopping. The sight of one chop, a small packet of frozen peas and a small can of fruit salad can be very depressing. And it's just too easy to get into the habit of thinking, 'I won't bother to cook today—it's only for me.' This is fatal, not only for one's health—appearance and vitality will suffer too.

Food for good health

Good food is one of the best investments for good health. The essential nutrients which the body must have are:

Protein, fat, carbohydrate, minerals and vitamins. The fat and carbohydrates tend to take care of themselves: bread, flour, sugar and butter, these are no problem. It is the protein, minerals and vitamins that seem to get left out, particularly by young people living alone in a flatlet for the first time, or by old people who are trying to manage on a small income or who find that some foods are difficult to eat. Two meals a day, each containing meat or fish or cheese or eggs, will supply the day's requirement of protein. You will find chapters of recipes for meat, fish and eggs in this book. There is no special mention of cheese—it is used in many of the recipes. But since cheese makes a perfect meal without requiring any cooking it is only sufficient to remember that it is a value source of protein. Two ounces of cheese provides about a fifth of the body's protein needs for the whole day.

Cheese with fruit, in a salad of raw vegetables, as an accompaniment to fruit pie or fruit cake —there is no problem about ways of serving it. And if you haven't already tried it have a chunk of Cheddar cheese with hot buttered toast and marmalade for breakfast.

The essential vitamins are found in the following foods and these could be taken into consideration when planning meals.

Iron: liver, kidney, bacon, ham, green vegetables, especially spinach, dried fruits including apricots, prunes and dates, eggs, black treacle and molasses, fish and shell fish.

Vitamin B complex: milk and milk products, eggs, cheese, liver and offal, fish and shell fish, green vegetables, tomatoes and other fruits, peas and beans, wholewheat bread.

Vitamin A: itself contained in butter and margarine, in liver, and in fat fish like herring and pilchard.

Vitamin C: tomatoes, oranges, lemons, grapefruit and blackcurrant.

A generous intake of the Vitamin B complex is essential for the 'full of beans' feeling that makes life worth living. The easiest way to ensure this is to eat natural wheat germ. Two or three spoonfuls sprinkled on cereal at breakfast time or on yoghourt or stewed fruit will make a delicious and nutritious addition to the day's meals and it is not expensive.

There is another aspect to the difficulties of cooking for one—lack of cooking facilities. This also contributes largely to this 'can't be bothered to cook' feeling. There are a variety of small cookers and refrigerators on the market and if you have a flat equipped with either or both of these appliances you will find that catering for yourself is really not so difficult. But if you have only a gas ring—or a gas ring and grill—then you cannot be blamed for thinking that cooking a well-balanced meal is impossible.

Don't lose heart—it is quite a challenge but it can be done. Start off with a few simple recipes from this book and the suggestions for making the best use of the cooking facilities that are available and you'll be surprised at the number of good meals that you can prepare.

In this book you will not find many of the traditional recipes since there are endless numbers of books containing these. The recipes have been chosen to cater for the particular problems of the person who, for most of the time, is cooking for one. However, since there is sure to be an occasion when you would like to serve home-made cake or biscuits or pastry that you have made yourself, some of these recipes have been included.

Some Useful Facts and Figures

Notes on metrication

In case you wish to convert quantities into metric measures, the following tables give a comparison.

Solid measures

Ounces	Approx. grams to nearest whole figure	Recommended conversion to nearest unit of 25
1	28	25
2	57	50
3	85	75
4	113	100
5	142	150
6	170	175
7	198	200
8	227	225
9	255	250
10	283	275
11	312	300
12	340	350
13	368	375
14	396	400
15	425	425
16 (1 lb)	454	450

Note: When converting quantities over 20 oz first add the appropriate figures in the centre column, then adjust to the nearest unit of 25. As a general guide, 1 kg (1000 g) equals 2·2 lb or about 2 lb 3 oz. This method of conversion gives good results in nearly all cases, although in certain pastry and cake recipes a more accurate conversion is necessary to produce a balanced recipe.

Liquid measures

Imperial	Approx. millilitres to nearest whole figure	Recommended millilitres
$\frac{1}{4}$ pint	142	150
$\frac{1}{2}$ pint	283	300
$\frac{3}{4}$ pint	425	450
1 pint	567	600
1$\frac{1}{2}$ pints	851	900
1$\frac{3}{4}$ pints	992	1000 (1 litre)

Oven temperatures

The table below gives recommended equivalents.

	°C	°F	Gas Mark
Very cool	110	225	$\frac{1}{4}$
	120	250	$\frac{1}{2}$
Cool	140	275	1
	150	300	2
Moderate	160	325	3
	180	350	4
Moderately hot	190	375	5
	200	400	6
Hot	220	425	7
	230	450	8
Very hot	240	475	9

Notes for American and Australian users

In America the 8-oz measuring cup is used. In Australia metric measures are now used in conjunction with the standard 250-ml measuring cup. The Imperial pint, used in Britain and Australia, is 20 fl oz, while the American pint is 16 fl oz. It is important to remember that the Australian tablespoon differs from both the British and American tablespoons; the table below gives a comparison. The British standard tablespoon, which has been used throughout this book, holds 17·7 ml, the American 14·2 ml, and the Australian 20 ml. A teaspoon holds approximately 5 ml in all three countries.

Shopping for one

Quantities to allow

The amounts given below are approximate quantities to allow for one meal for one person:

Meat

Without bone	...	...	4–6 oz.
With bone	...	...	6–8 oz.
For made up dishes	...	...	2–3 oz.

Fish

Without bone	...	...	3–5 oz.
With much bone	...	...	6 oz.
For made up dishes	...	...	2–3 oz.

Vegetables, weight as purchased

Beans (broad)	...	...	8 oz.
Beans (runner)	...	...	6 oz.
Brussels sprouts	...	...	6 oz.
Cabbage	...	...	8 oz.
Celery...	...	...	¼ large head or 1 small head
Carrots	...	...	4 oz.
Greens (spring)	...	...	8 oz.
Onions (as a vegetable)	...	6 oz.
Parsnips	...	...	6 oz.
Peas (green) ...	...	...	8 oz.
Potatoes	...	...	4–6 oz.
Spinach	...	...	8 oz.
Turnips	...	...	8 oz.

Puddings

Sponge and suet puddings ...	1½ oz. flour, etc.
Pastry (for pies and puddings)	1½ oz. flour, etc.
Milk puddings, moulds, jellies	¼ pint milk, etc.
Batter	1 oz. flour
Fruit (pies, puddings, stewed)	4–5 oz. fruit
Custard, as sauce ...	⅛ pint milk

Cereals

Rice (for curry, etc.)	...	1–1½ oz.
Macaroni	...	...	1–1½ oz.

Beverages

Tea ...	...	...	1 teaspoon
Sauces and gravies	...	...	⅛ pint

Convenience foods

A 'bachelor' cook will often find it cheaper and certainly easier to use convenience foods.

Canned or packet soups are a useful addition to the food cupboard. Use half as a first course or snack, the other half as a sauce with meat or fish, or as a gravy or the stock for a stew or casserole. The condensed soups are particularly good used in this way; diluted with 2 or 3 tablespoons of milk, they make a delicious sauce, filling for an omelette, or, with a beaten egg added, an individual pie filling.

Dried onions, seasoned salt and pepper and dried mixed herbs and lemon juice in plastic containers are all good buys. They last a long time and can be used to give extra flavour without any trouble. Small packets of frozen fish, meat and vegetables can be economical too, since there is no waste. 'Boil in the bag' rice, sauce mixes and pastry mixes or frozen pastry can be used to make some first class meals no matter how restricted your cooking facilities are.

A guide to can sizes

A table of the most common sizes, with approximate weight, with the name by which they are known to the trade (given in brackets), number of servings and types of food packed in the various sizes is given here as a guide.

Approx. net weight	Approx. number of servings	Used principally for
5 oz.	1	Baked beans, peas
8 oz.	2	Fruit salad, fruits
8 oz.	2	Meat puddings, meats, baked beans, spaghetti, vegetables, fruit.
10 oz. (A.1)	2–3	Baked beans, soups, vegetables, meats, pilchards
14 oz. (E.1)	3	Fruits, vegetables
1 lb.	4	Vegetables, fruit, meat,

(No. 1 tall)		soups, pilchards, milk, cream, fruit juices, spaghetti, milk pudding	$1\frac{1}{4}$ lb. (A.2)	4	Fruit, fruit salad, vegetables, fruit and vegetable juices
1 lb.	4	Sweet and meat puddings, tongue, galantine	$1\frac{3}{4}$ lb. (A.2½)	5–6	Fruit and vegetables

Storing food

Bread

Keep bread in a bread bin or wrapped in a dry cloth or polythene bag. A bread bin should have holes in the lid or some other form of ventilation or the bread may rapidly develop mould. Bread should never be put away whilst warm as this encourages mould by making the container damp. Avoid collecting scraps of bread in the bottom of the bin and clean it out regularly. If bread does go mouldy, scald out the container with boiling water and dry thoroughly before use.

Eggs

These have porous shells and should be kept away from strong smelling foods. Place in a bowl or egg rack and leave in the carton if supplied in one. Shelled eggs should be covered and used as soon as possible.

Fats

Keep fats away from foods with a strong flavour or they may become tainted. Dripping should be stored in a covered basin. It will become rancid more quickly if exposed to light.

Fish

Place fish in a covered dish until ready for use, to prevent the smell from flavouring other food.

Fruit

Spread out fruit on a shallow dish or rack in a cool airy place.

Meat

Place meat on a grid with a plate underneath it to allow air to circulate freely round it. Cover loosely with greaseproof paper or a ventilated meat cover. Never leave meat tightly wrapped.

Milk

If the larder is not cool, stand the bottle or jug in cold water. Cover with a piece of clean damp muslin with the ends of the muslin in the water. If this is placed in a draught the water will evaporate and so cool the milk.

Vegetables

To keep celery and cucumber fresh, place in 2–3 inches of water, stalk end down. Change the water daily. Most other vegetables will keep in a well ventilated vegetable rack or box in a cool dark corner of the larder or kitchen. When it is necessary to store green vegetables every effort should be made to keep them fresh and crisp. Wash but do not soak lettuce, shake off the water and keep in a covered saucepan or polythene bag. Unwashed lettuce, cauliflower, beans, etc., can be kept for a few days in a covered container or wrapped tightly in paper or a polythene bag.

Dried fruit

If stored in a jar without a tightly fitting lid these can be stored for up to one year. Avoid dampness or the fruit may go mouldy.

Essences, herbs, spices and seasonings

Buy in small quantities and keep tightly covered to preserve aroma and flavour. Spices and seasonings include such commodities as mustard, pepper, peppercorns, etc. Protect herbs from light to conserve colour.

Sugar, gelatine, jellies and custard powder

These keep almost indefinitely if stored in the packet, in an airtight tin in a dry place.

Cheese

If cheese is sold in a box or tinfoil wrapper, keep it in this, otherwise wrap in greased or waxed paper or place it in a cheese dish with a ventilated cover. Keep vacuum packed cheese in the wrapper until required.

Cereals

These may be stored in jars or tins with tightly fitted lids. Flour may go musty after several months. Oatmeal and wholemeal have a limited storage life. Other cereals will keep for approximately one year.

Cooking on a Gas Ring

Equipment

One of the greatest difficulties of cooking in a bed-sitter or flatlet is lack of space and this is made more complicated when the only 'cookery' is the gas ring on the floor by the fire. A white wood trolley is a good investment if the 'housekeeping' can be stretched to buy it. Use it for keeping all your cooking equipment and china together. It will also be invaluable for entertaining.

If you cannot afford a trolley, have a strong wooden box (an orange box on its side will do), as near the gas ring as possible. Cover the box with a gay, self-adhesive covering, invest in a plastic cutlery tray and you have the basis for your 'kitchen unit'. A strong tray is useful and a small bread board which can also be used as a chopping board; add a washing up bowl and some storage boxes or jars and you can consider that you are quite well equipped.

The following list of equipment will provide the basic 'tools' for the job of preparing a good meal and can be added to according to your needs—and budget.

2–3 small saucepans	One should have a well-fitting lid
1 kettle	An electric kettle is a real boon if you can afford one since it provides an additional source of hot water
1 baking sheet or roasting tin	Useful for putting hot pans on
2 oven glass basins	One large enough for mixing, one which will fit on the top of a saucepan
1 1-pint jug ...	A measuring jug is most useful
1 frying pan ...	If you can afford two pans, an omelette pan is a most useful buy.

1 colander or strainer
1–2 wooden spoons
1 small sharp knife
1 large metal spoon
1 fork
1 bread knife
1 set measuring spoons
1 can opener
1 5-inch ovenglass plate

Making the Best use of a Gas Ring

Wrap beans, peas or carrots in aluminium foil and cook in the pan with potatoes.

Cook an extra vegetable (see above) at lunch time. Serve with cheese sauce for supper.

To keep food hot (e.g. egg custard, cooked rice), place in a small basin, cover with saucepan lid or foil. Place basin over pan of soup, stew, etc., while cooking or reheating the latter. Additional food can be kept hot in a jug, standing in a pan of boiling water off the heat. To warm plates place them on the jug until required.

Guide to Shallow Frying

Food	Amount of fat or oil to use	Approximate frying time
Chops, fillet steak	about 1 dessert-spoon	1 inch thick, 2–4 minutes on each side; 1½ inches thick, 3–5 minutes on each side.
Bacon	about 1 dessert-spoon or less	½–1 minute on each side
Pancakes and fritters	about 1 dessert-spoon or less	3–4 minutes, fry on each side until golden
Sausages	about 1 dessert-spoon	15–20 minutes according to size. Turn frequently
Fish	5–6 tablespoons	3–10 minutes on each side, according to thickness
Fish cakes, fish sticks	about 5 table-spoons	2–8 minutes on each side, according to size
Liver	about 5 table-spoons	2–4 minutes on each side
Onions	about 5 table-spoons or if pre-ferred 1–2 table-spoons and after lightly browning, cover and reduce the heat	Until golden brown and tender
Sauté potatoes	5–6 tablespoons	If parboiled, 3–4 minutes over moderate heat. If raw, 9–10 minutes over very low heat
Eggs	2–3 tablespoons	1–3 minutes, according to taste
Cheaper cuts of steaks and hamburgers	5–6 tablespoons	8–10 minutes on each side
Spring chicken joints; if frozen, defrost and dry before frying	5–6 tablespoons	Brown for 5 minutes on each side. Cover, lower heat and cook a further 5–10 minutes on each side

Cooking on a Grill

Tomatoes and mushrooms: Smear with butter or baste with fat and cook in the pan or on the grid as convenient. Season tomatoes with pepper, salt and sugar. If they are cooked whole, the skin should be cut round the top. Allow 7–15 minutes. For mushrooms allow at least 10 minutes.

Liver: Sliced calves' or lambs' liver is suitable for grilling. Wash and dry well. Heat some cooking or bacon fat in the grill pan and turn the liver in the hot fat. Allow about 3 minutes on either side. If liver is over-cooked it becomes hard. Allow 4–6 oz. for 1 generous serving.

Kidney: Lambs' kidneys are considered best for grilling. Pigs' kidneys can also be used. Slit the kidney on the rounded side and cut out the core with kitchen scissors. Wash and dry and treat as for liver, allowing about 10 minutes cooking time. For a main dish allow 2 lambs' kidneys per person or 1½ pigs' kidneys.

Sausages: Prick well and cook on the grid. Turn several times during cooking. For large pork sausages allow at least 15 minutes' grilling. When the sausages are browned reduce the heat to medium or low to ensure thorough cooking without over-browning. Allow 2 sausages per person.

Mutton and lamb cutlets: Cut off surplus fat. Scrape the front of the cutlet bone and trim away meat and fat from the end of the bone. Brush with a little oil or melted fat and cook under a hot grill, turning the cutlet as soon as the first side is browned. For mutton cutlets allow 10–12 minutes and allow 1 per person. For lamb cutlets allow 7–8 minutes and allow 2 per person.

Chops: Trim off surplus fat. Brush with a little oil or melted fat under a hot grill until both sides are browned. If very thick reduce heat to 'medium' to cook the chops through. Turn twice during cooking. Allow 12–15 minutes' grilling. Allow 1 chop per person.

Pork chops: Put on the grid and cook under a hot grill until both sides are browned. Turn twice during cooking. If necessary reduce heat to medium after browning to ensure that the chops are well cooked. Allow at least 15 minutes' grilling. Allow 1 chop per person.

Veal: This is a lean meat and needs protection from the fierce heat of the grill. Coat in egg and breadcrumbs, to which a little grated cheese may be added if liked. Cook in the grill pan and baste well with butter, or bacon fat. Cutlets of veal or thin pieces of fillet of veal can be used for grilling. Cook each side until golden brown. Allow about 10 minutes. Allow 1–2 cutlets per person and 3–5 oz. of fillet per person.
Veal is usually served with an accompaniment to give extra flavour. For example: a rasher of bacon or two fillets of anchovy and a few capers or a slice of lemon.

Mixed grill

This consists of a piece of steak or a chop or two cutlets and two or more of the following: kidney, liver, sausage, bacon rasher, mushrooms, tomatoes—the whole garnished with watercress and maître d'hôtel butter (page 71) and served with chipped or mashed potatoes or hot potato crisps.

Bacon and eggs

With a sharp knife or the kitchen scissors trim off the rind and 'rust' from the bacon rasher. Clip the fat two or three times to keep the rasher a good shape while cooking. Put the rasher on the grid to allow the fat to drop away from it. Cook under a well heated grill for about 3–5 minutes, depending on the thickness of the rasher. All but very thin rashers will need turning halfway through the cooking.

To cook eggs: Heat some cooking or bacon fat in the grill pan. Break the eggs separately into a cup or saucer and slide these into the hot fat. Place the bacon on the grid over the eggs and put the pan under the grill. The bacon fat will help to baste the eggs. When the bacon is cooked, remove the grid and finish cooking the eggs with the grill turned low.

Fried Bread: When serving with bacon try to use bacon fat. Heat some fat in the grill pan. Dip the slices of bread in the fat and then put them on the grid and put this in the grill pan. When the first slice is crisp, turn the slice over and brown the second side.

En brochette

This consists of skewering small pieces of food on a skewer. Special flat skewers are ideal but if these are not available, twisted metal skewers as used by butchers will be found fairly satisfactory.
A suitable choice of foods might be chipolata sausage, a small tomato, a bacon roll, a small flat mushroom and a strip of thin steak 1½ inches long and 1 inch wide. Brush with oil or melted bacon fat or butter and grill for 10–12 minutes, turning frequently.

Joints of small roasting chicken

Wipe and trim the joints. Rub with soft butter or bacon fat, then put in the grill pan. Heat grill thoroughly and start by cooking the flesh side first. After 4 minutes change to the skin side and after 2 minutes change back to the flesh side. Repeat this throughout cooking. After about 15 minutes reduce the heat to medium. Allow 30 minutes' cooking time. Remove from the grill, spread with softened butter and sprinkle with salt.
For additional flavour, prior to cooking sprinkle on a few drops of lemon juice or rub on a few grains of ground ginger or curry powder. Then rub with fat as above.

Grilling fish

Kippers: Remove head and tail and trim fins. Cook skin side for 1 minute then turn, brush with melted butter and finish cooking on the flesh side. Allow about 5 minutes. Allow 1 or 2 per person. Alternatively wrap each kipper in greaseproof paper. Lay the fleshy side in the centre of the paper and fold neatly with the ends coming over the skin side. Place in the grill pan with the flesh side uppermost. Heat the grill at high then turn to medium whilst grilling the kippers for about 7 minutes. Slit the paper, remove the kippers to the serving dish and carefully throw away the cooking paper.

Herrings: Gut the fish and remove head, tail and trim fins. With the point of a sharp knife make 3 or 4 incisions in the thick part of the flesh on both sides of the backbone. Place the fish on the grid and grill for about 4 minutes on the first side. Turn and finish cooking on the second side. Allow 10 12 minutes' grilling. Serve with a thick slice of lemon and or mustard sauce. Allow 1 2 herrings per person.

Trout: Gut the fish, remove the eyes and trim the tail and fins. Brush with butter or oil and grill in the pan for about 4 minutes on the first side. Turn, rebrush with fat and finish cooking on the second side. Allow 10 12 minutes' grilling. Serve with a thick slice of lemon and melted butter and chopped parsley or with maître d'hôtel butter (page 71). Allow 1 2 per person.

Grilling white fish

The flesh of white fish tears easily and for this reason it is recommended that this type of fish should always be cooked in the grill pan and not on the grid. Cutlets and steaks of fish which need turning during cooking should be turned before the fish is half cooked as later it is more likely to break. As white fish contains little fat it is necessary to add fat during cooking and to serve the fish with melted butter or maître d'hôtel butter unless grilled with cheese or served with an accompanying sauce or served with grilled bacon.

Before grilling the fish should be washed and dried very well. When necessary it should be trimmed. White fish may be sprinkled with lemon juice and a little pepper before grilling. Salt should be sprinkled on before grilling is complete.

Turbot and halibut: For cutlets and steaks place in the greased grill pan and brush the fish with oil or melted butter. Cook under a hot grill for about 4 minutes. Then turn, re-brush and continue cooking on other side. Allow about 10 minutes' grilling. Allow about 3 5 oz. per person.

Fillets of white fish: Cod, hake, whiting, bream, plaice and sole. If it is desired to skin the fillet start from the tail end and, firmly holding the skin, slide a sharp knife between skin and flesh. Place in the greased grill pan, brush with melted butter or oil and grill about 5 6 minutes without turning. Baste or re-brush with fat if the fish becomes dry. Allow 3 5 oz. per person.

Alternatively toss in flour, shake most of the flour off, then coat in beaten egg and breadcrumbs. Place in the greased grill pan and add flakes of butter or margarine on top of the fish, and sprinkle with finely grated cheese. Brush with melted butter and sprinkle lightly with browned crumbs.

Cod and hake cutlets: Treat in any of the ways suggested for fillets of fish but turn after about 4 minutes and allow 10 12 minutes' grilling in all. Allow about 4 6 oz. per person.

Fish cakes (see recipe on page 22): Melt some butter, cooking or bacon fat in the grill pan. Dip one side of each fish cake in the melted fat and lay the other side in the pan. Grill till brown on the first side then turn, add a nut of margarine and brown second side. Allow about 10 minutes.

Main meals with meat and fish

Pot roasting

This is the ideal method of cooking small joints. Allow 40 minutes per lb. for thin joints, 45 minutes per lb. for thick or rolled joints. ·

1 Melt enough dripping to cover the bottom of a pan. It should be a heavy saucepan with a well-fitting lid.
2 When the fat is very hot, put the joint in and brown it well all over.
3 Reduce heat, cover and cook slowly, allowing 40–45 minutes to the lb. according to thickness until tender.
4 Place the meat, after browning, on a rack if available or on 2–3 skewers* in the bottom of the pan. If the joint is very lean, baste it occasionally during cooking. Prepared root vegetables and potatoes may be cooked round the meat.
*to prevent the joint from sticking.

Minute steak

cooking time 10 minutes
you will need:
1 small fillet steak (weighing approximately 4 oz.)
¼ oz. butter
1 dessertspoonful Worcestershire sauce
1 small packet frozen broccoli
½ packet potato crisps

1 Put frozen broccoli on to cook in boiling water according to instructions on the packet.
2 Empty potato crisps in to an ovenproof dish and place in warm oven to heat through.
3 Beat steak until only ⅛ inch thick all over.
4 Heat a thick frying pan and when very hot add butter and the Worcestershire sauce.
5 Add the steak immediately, cooking it for 30 seconds on either side. Reduce heat and continue cooking until steak is tender.
6 Serve at once with vegetables and crisps.

Austrian steak

cooking time 15 minutes
you will need:

4 oz. rump steak cut very thin	horseradish sauce
2 large mushrooms	watercress
1 oz. butter	potato crisps

1 Melt butter in a frying pan. When beginning to brown add the steak.
2 Brown on both sides and cook until it is as tender as required (about 5–10 minutes).

3 When nearly cooked add mushrooms.
4 Remove steak to a warm dish. Garnish with mushrooms, placing a little horseradish in each.
5 If liked add 2–3 tablespoons wine to the pan, bring to the boil and pour over the steak.
6 Serve with potato crisps and watercress.

Hamburger steak

cooking time about 10 minutes
you will need:

4–6 oz. lean rump steak, minced	good pinch salt
1 oz. butter	pinch pepper
½ small egg	pinch grated nutmeg
1 oz. butter for garnishing	1 Spanish onion

1 Peel the onion and cut into thick rings. Cook gently in butter until a pale golden brown. Keep hot.
2 Lightly mix the minced steak with the seasoning and beaten egg and form lightly into 2–3 flattish cakes.
3 Butter the grill pan, put in the meat cakes and cook for about 5 minutes on either side under a hot grill.
4 Sprinkle with salt, dot with butter and serve hot with the onion rings.
To 'halve' an egg, break the egg into a cup or saucer and beat with a fork, just enough to mix yolk and white. Measure out with a spoon as required. 1 large egg gives about 3 tablespoons beaten egg.

Stewed steak and kidney

cooking time 1 hour
you will need:

8 oz. stewing steak	1 good pinch mixed herbs
1 large onion	½ can kidney soup
1 dessertspoon dripping	⅛ pint water

1 Cut the steak into 1-inch cubes. Peel and slice the onion.
2 Fry the steak in the dripping until browned all over. Remove and fry the onion until lightly browned.
3 Return the meat to the pan and stir in the dried herbs, soup and water.
4 Bring to the boil, reduce heat, cover and simmer until meat is tender.
5 This makes a generous meal for one; half the cooked steak can be used to make a tasty pie. (See recipe for individual pie, page 67).

Steak and tomato casserole
cooking time about 2 hours

you will need:

4–6 oz. stewing steak	1 tablespoon tomato purée
$\frac{1}{2}$ oz. seasoned flour	$\frac{1}{4}$ pint stock or water

1 Remove any excess fat and gristle from the steak and cut into 1-inch cubes.
2 Coat the steak with seasoned flour.
3 Place in a casserole with the stock or water and tomato purée.
4 Cook in a slow oven (290° F.—Gas Mark 1) until tender.

Creamed beef
cooking time about 45 minutes

you will need:

4 oz. minced beef	$\frac{1}{4}$ pint milk
1 heaped dessertspoon cornflour	$\frac{1}{4}$ pint water
1 dessertspoon corn oil	1–2 potatoes
1 small onion	seasoning

1 Toss beef in cornflour.
2 Heat oil in saucepan, add the onion, chopped or grated, and the beef.
3 Cook until oil is absorbed, about 3 minutes.
4 Stir in the water and milk and bring to the boil, reduce heat and cook gently until the meat is almost tender, about 30 minutes.
5 Add the diced potato and cook for a further 15 minutes. Taste and add more seasoning if necessary.

If preferred omit potato and serve with boiled rice or fingers of toast.

One dish meal
cooking time 45 minutes

you will need:

$\frac{1}{2}$ oz. dripping	4 tablespoons tomato soup
4–6 oz. minced steak	4 oz. peeled and sliced
1 small onion, sliced finely	potato

1 Melt the dripping and fry the minced meat until evenly browned, stirring all the time.
2 Add the onion and cook for about 5 minutes.
3 Add the soup to the mixture, stirring well.
4 Arrange half the potatoes in the bottom of a shallow ovenproof dish.
5 Cover with the meat mixture, arrange the remaining potato sliced over the top. Cover with buttered paper.
6 Bake in a moderately hot oven (375° F.—Gas Mark 5) until meat is tender and potato is browned.

Chilli con carne
cooking time about 1 hour

you will need:

8 oz. minced beef	$\frac{1}{4}$–$\frac{1}{2}$ teaspoon chilli powder
1 small onion	$\frac{1}{2}$ level teaspoon salt
1 small can peeled tomatoes	good pinch cayenne pepper
1 bay leaf	good pinch paprika
	1 small can baked beans

1 Cook the beef in a pan without any additional fat until beginning to brown.
2 Add the finely chopped onion and cook for 5 minutes.
3 Add the tomatoes and seasonings, bring to the boil and cover.
4 Simmer gently until meat is tender and flavours matured.
5 Add the beans and reheat. Remove the bay leaf and serve.
Any left-over mixture can be served on toast, sprinkled with a little cheese and grilled, or used as a filling for a small meat pasty.

Roast stuffed breast of lamb
cooking time 1 hour

you will need:

1 small boned breast of lamb	good pinch mixed herbs
4 oz. fresh white breadcrumbs	1 large tomato, chopped
grated rind and juice $\frac{1}{2}$ lemon	1 egg, beaten
	2 oz. lard

1 Wipe the lamb and sprinkle with salt and pepper.
2 Mix the breadcrumbs, lemon rind and juice and mixed herbs together.
3 Add the egg and mix until well blended.
4 Spread the stuffing over the lamb, roll up and tie securely.
5 Place in a roasting tin and dot with the lard.
6 Roast in the centre of a moderately hot oven (375° F.—Gas Mark 5) until meat is tender and crisp and golden on the outside.

Curried lamb chop
cooking time 25–30 minutes

you will need:

1–2 lamb chops	$\frac{1}{4}$ oz. flour
1 oz. butter or margarine	$\frac{1}{4}$ pint stock
1 small onion, chopped	salt and pepper
$\frac{1}{2}$ cooked apple, peeled and cored	1 small can curried beans

1 Heat the butter or margarine and fry the chops until browned on both sides. Remove from the pan.

2 Add the onion and the apple, sliced, to the pan and fry over a low heat for about 5 minutes.
3 Sprinkle with flour, cook a further 3 minutes, then add the stock.
4 Bring to the boil, stirring all the time. Lower the heat and season to taste.
5 Add the chops, cover and simmer until tender.
6 When the chops are cooked, add the beans and cook for 5 minutes, stirring carefully.
7 Serve with French bread.

Curried mutton

cooking time 1½ hours

you will need:

8 oz. breast or neck of mutton	½ oz. fat
1 small onion	1 level teaspoon curry powder
2–3 tomatoes	good pinch salt
2 oz. Patna rice	

1 Cut the meat into 1-inch cubes.
2 Peel and slice the onion and tomatoes.
3 Heat the fat in a saucepan or casserole and fry the onions until they are golden in colour.
4 Add the curry powder and salt and then the meat and continue frying until the meat is browned.
5 Add the tomatoes and a little water if it seems necessary.
6 Simmer until the meat is tender adding more water if needed.
7 Serve with boiled rice.

Lamb curry using remainders

cooking time 40 minutes

you will need:

1 oz. butter	4–6 oz. cooked lamb
1 medium onion	¼ pint tomato juice
1 level tablespoon curry powder	1 level teaspoon salt
	1 tablespoon lemon juice

1 Peel and chop the onion, squeeze the lemon juice.
2 Remove any fat and skin from the lamb and cut into small pieces.
3 Melt the butter and fry the onion until golden.
4 Add the curry powder and mix well.
5 Add the meat and fry for 2–3 minutes, stirring frequently.
6 Add the tomato juice and simmer for 30 minutes.
7 Add the salt and lemon juice and serve hot with boiled rice.

Braised cutlets

cooking time about 40 minutes

you will need:

1 small onion	1 lump sugar
1–2 lamb cutlets	little water
1 young turnip	4 oz. shelled green peas
seasoning	creamed potato or boiled rice

1 Slice the onion very thinly and place in a fire-proof casserole.
2 Wipe and trim the cutlets and lay them on top.
3 Add the turnip, cut into small dice, the seasoning and sugar.
4 Add just enough water to nearly cover the contents.
5 Cover and cook at (375° F.—Gas Mark 5) for 20 minutes.
6 Add the peas and cook for a further 20 minutes.
7 Serve very hot, accompanied by creamed potato or rice.

Winter pie

cooking time about 1½ hours

you will need:

2–3 oz. suet pastry	seasoning
4–6 oz. stewing steak	½ tablespoon flour
2 small carrots	1 oz. dripping
1 small onion	about ½ pint hot water
2–3 tomatoes	

1 Wipe the meat and cut into cubes, removing skin and gristle.
2 Mix flour with salt and pepper and toss the meat in this.
3 Heat the dripping in a small pan and fry the meat until brown.
4 Peel the carrots and onion and cut into slices. Skin and chop the tomatoes.
5 Add the vegetables to the meat, mix well and add enough water to cover. Put a lid on the pan and simmer for about 1 hour, stirring occasionally, until the meat is almost tender.
6 Meanwhile, roll out the suet pastry and, using the lid of the pan, cut out a round to fit the top of the pan.
7 Place the pastry 'lid' on, resting it on the contents of the pan.
8 Replace the pan lid and cook for a further 30 minutes until pastry has risen to the pan lid.
9 Serve the pie, at once, from the pan.

Lamb Creole

cooking time 30-45 minutes

you will need:

1 or 2 loin chops	salt and pepper
flour	½ can condensed tomato
½ oz. butter or dripping	soup
1 small onion, finely	1 level teaspoon chopped
chopped	dried rosemary

1 Trim excess fat from the chops, season with salt and pepper and coat lightly with flour.
2 Melt the butter or dripping and fry the onion until beginning to colour.
3 Push the onion to one side of the pan and quickly fry the chops until brown.
4 Place the chops and onion in a casserole, pour the condensed soup over. Sprinkle with rosemary.
5 Cover and bake in a very moderate oven (335° F. Gas Mark 3) until chops are tender.
6 Serve with Patna rice.

Veal stew

cooking time about 40 minutes

you will need:

4 oz. stewing veal	salt and pepper
½ oz. butter	¼ pint milk
1 small onion	4 bacon rolls
½ oz. flour	

1 Cut the veal into 1-inch cubes, fry in the butter and add the onion cut into rings.
2 Stir in the flour and seasoning. Cook for 3 minutes.
3 Add the milk, bring to boil, reduce heat and simmer for 30 minutes.
4 Serve with bacon rolls. To make these, cut 2 rashers streaky bacon in half. Roll up and grill until crisp.

Neck of veal with forcemeat balls

cooking time 1½ hours

you will need:

8 oz. neck of veal	½ oz. fat
1 small onion	¼ oz. flour
½ carrot	¼ pint stock
veal force meat (see	good pinch salt
page 71)	pinch pepper

1 Have the veal cut into joints.
2 Peel and slice the onion and carrot.
3 Make the forcemeat balls while the meat is cooking.
4 Heat the fat in a pan or casserole and fry the veal until brown.
5 Remove the meat and fry the vegetables.

6 Sprinkle in the flour, mix and cook for 1-2 minutes.
7 Stir in stock, bring to the boil and add seasoning and meat.
8 Cover and simmer until tender, adding the forcemeat balls during the last 30 minutes of cooking.

Stuffed ox liver

cooking time 1 hour

you will need:

4 oz. ox liver	2 rashers streaky bacon
2 level tablespoons	stock
stuffing, or veal	
forcemeat (see page 71)	

1 Wash liver well in warm water.
2 Cut out any tubes and fat, remove the skin.
3 Slice thinly and arrange in a shallow dish.
4 Pour 4 tablespoons boiling water on the stuffing if using packet and soak for a few minutes, or make the veal forcemeat.
5 Remove bacon rinds, chop one rasher finely and mix with the stuffing.
6 Spread this on top of the liver and cover with remaining rasher.
7 Moisten with a little stock.
8 Cover and bake in a moderately hot oven (375° F.—Gas Mark 5) until the liver is tender and the bacon cooked—about 1 hour.
9 Serve with creamed potatoes.

Lamb with rice

cooking time 1 hour

you will need:

8 oz. lean lamb without	1 tablespoon oil
bone	½ level teaspoon salt
1 small onion	⅛ level teaspoon pepper
3 tablespoons tomato paste	2–3 oz. Patna rice
¼ pint water	

1 Cut the meat into 1-inch cubes.
2 Peel and slice the onion, blend the tomato paste and water.
3 Heat the oil in a deep frying pan or shallow saucepan.
4 Brown the lamb in it for about 8 minutes.
5 Add the onion, cover and simmer until the onion is soft, about 10 minutes.
6 Add salt and pepper and the tomato mixture.
7 Cover and cook gently for about 45 minutes or until the meat is tender.
8 Meanwhile, boil the rice and drain well.
9 Heap the rice on a hot plate and spoon the lamb mixture into the centre.
This makes sufficient for 2 servings. Reheat in small pan, adding a good knob of butter.

Risotto

cooking time about 40 minutes

you will need:

2 rashers streaky bacon	2 oz. Patna rice
½ oz. lard	salt and pepper
2 oz. mushroom stalks	2–3 drops Worcestershire
1 large tomato, skinned	sauce
and chopped	1 teaspoon tomato purée
1 small onion, finely	1 chicken stock cube
chopped	½ pint hot water

Remove the rind from the bacon and cut each rasher into small pieces.

Melt the fat and fry the bacon pieces until crisp. Remove from the heat and add the washed mushroom stalks.

Add the tomato and onion to the pan and cook for about 3 minutes.

Add the rice, mix well, and add the tomato purée and Worcestershire sauce.

Add the stock cube to the water, stir until dissolved and pour into the pan.

Cook gently until the rice is tender and all the liquid has been absorbed.

Season lightly to taste and serve at once.

Lamb cutlets in orange sauce

cooking time about 30–40 minutes

you will need:

1 oz. lard	¼ pint water
4 best end of neck cutlets	grated rind 1 orange
2 level dessertspoons	2 level teaspoons sugar
seasoned flour	1 level tablespoon flour
juice 2 oranges (¼ pint)	parsley

1 Roll the cutlets in seasoned flour and brown in the lard. Pour off any excess fat.

2 Add the orange juice and water and simmer slowly until tender.

3 Remove the cutlets and keep hot.

4 Blend the orange rind, sugar and flour together and add the orange liquor. Stir well and cook for a few minutes.

5 Replace the cutlets in the orange sauce and heat through.

6 Serve hot garnished with parsley.
Enough for 2 servings.

Spaghetti Bolognese

cooking time 40 minutes

you will need:

2 tablespoons oil	salt and pepper
1 onion	½ pint stock (can be made
8 oz. raw minced beef	with a stock cube)
2 level tablespoons flour	2 tablespoons sherry, red
1 tablespoon tomato purée	wine or cider (optional)
or 2 skinned chopped	4 oz. spaghetti
tomatoes	3–4 oz. grated cheese

1 Heat the oil in a saucepan and add peeled and finely chopped onion (and if liked half a clove of chopped garlic). Fry gently until soft but not brown.

2 Add the meat and fry, stirring for 2 minutes.

3 Remove from heat and mix in flour, tomato purée or chopped skinned tomatoes, the seasoning and stock and, if used, the wine or sherry.

4 Return to the heat and bring just to the boil, cover and simmer for about 30 minutes until the meat is cooked and the sauce is thick. If necessary add a little more liquid.

5 While the sauce is simmering, cook spaghetti in large pan of boiling salted water until just soft. Drain in colander.

6 Lift spaghetti on to a hot dish and fill centre with meat sauce mixture and sprinkle over the grated cheese.

7 If wished serve some extra grated cheese in a separate bowl.
Makes 2 good servings.
Note: True spaghetti Bolognese should be served with grated Parmesan cheese.

Stewed ox tail

cooking time 3¾ hours

you will need:

1 small ox tail	2 carrots
2 oz. plain flour	6 peppercorns
salt and pepper	1 sprig parsley
1 oz. lard	1 bay leaf (optional)
1 large onion, chopped	1 beef stock cube

1 Wash the ox tail and cut into neat thick pieces. Place in a pan and cover with cold water.

2 Bring to the boil, remove from the heat and drain off the water.

3 Dry the meat.

4 Season 1 oz. flour with salt and pepper and toss the meat in this.

5 Melt the lard and fry the meat until browned all over. Add the onion and fry until soft.

6 Scrape the carrots and cut each into four. Add to the pan. Add the remaining 1 oz. flour and mix well.

7 Tie the peppercorns, parsley and bay leaf if used in a piece of muslin and add to the pan.

8 Add 1 pint cold water and the beef stock cube.

9 Cover and bring to the boil, reduce the heat and simmer gently until tender. Re-season if necessary.
Makes enough for 2 good servings.

Boiled bacon

cooking time: pieces under 1 lb. allow 45 minutes
pieces of 1–2 lb. allow 1–1½ hours
over 3 lb. allow 30 minutes per lb.

cuts to use: top streaky, top back, short back, middle gammon, corner gammon, prime collar, prime streaky, back and ribs, long back and gammon hock are all suitable for boiling

For small pieces, soak about 1 hour in cold water to cover. Larger pieces 4 5 hours or longer if they are very salty.

1 Put in cold water to cover.
2 Bring slowly to the boil and remove any scum.
3 Add a peeled onion with 4 5 cloves stuck in it, or add 6 peppercorns and bay leaf.
4 Cover the bacon and simmer for the required time.
5 Vegetables may be added for the last 45 minutes of cooking time. Leave them in large pieces and choose from carrots, turnips, onions, potatoes and parsnips.
6 To serve hot, remove rind, sprinkle with browned crumbs and serve with vegetables.
7 If you wish to serve the bacon cold, omit the vegetables, remove the rind when joint is cooked. Replace joint in liquid in which it was cooked and leave until cold.

Fried fish

cooking time about 7 minutes

you will need:

2 cod fillets	1 level teaspoon chopped
1 beaten egg	parsley
browned breadcrumbs	1 tablespoon finely
salt and pepper	chopped cucumber
1 tablespoon mayonnaise	(optional)
	deep fat for frying

1 Wipe the fish and remove any bones, season with salt and pepper.
2 Dip the fish in egg, toss in breadcrumbs. Shake off any loose crumbs and repeat again.
3 Heat the fat in a deep pan and when hot enough, add the fish and fry until golden brown.
4 Meanwhile, make the sauce by mixing the mayonnaise, parsley and cucumber if used together. Season to taste.
5 Drain the fish on crumpled paper and serve at once with the sauce.

Oven fried fish

cooking time about 10 minutes, depending on thickness of fish

you will need:

2 fillets white fish	browned crumbs
seasoned flour	2 tablespoons oil
beaten egg	

1 Preheat oven to 400 F. —Gas Mark 6.
2 Dip fish in seasoned flour, brush with beaten egg and coat with browned breadcrumbs.
3 Heat enough oil to cover the bottom of a shallow baking dish and put in the pieces of fish. Baste with the hot oil and bake uncovered until tender.

Chicken joints, chops, liver, sausages, etc., may also be cooked by this method.

Baked fish

cooking time about 20 minutes

you will need:

1 steak or 4–6 oz. filleted	clove of garlic
fish	1 tablespoon chopped
¼ teaspoon pepper	parsley
½ teaspoon salt	½ oz. butter
1 teaspoon lemon juice	2 tomatoes
1 small onion	parsley to garnish

1 Wash and dry the fish (if fillets are used they should be skinned). Place the fish in a fireproof dish and sprinkle with pepper, salt and lemon juice.
2 Chop the onion and garlic finely and mix with the chopped parsley. Then fry in the butter.
3 Peel and slice the tomatoes, add one to the onion mixture and season lightly with the pepper and salt.
4 Cover the fish with the tomato mixture then with the remaining sliced tomato.
5 Dot with butter, cover and bake in a moderate oven (350 F. Gas Mark 4) for 10 15 minutes.

Spanish fish

cooking time 20–30 minutes

you will need:

1 oz. butter or margarine	1 tomato, skinned
1 Spanish onion	½ teaspoon castor sugar
1 steak or cutlet of cod	chopped parsley
salt, cayenne pepper	

1 Melt the butter or margarine in a large pan.
2 Slice the onion and fry lightly.
3 Place the fish on the onion and season to taste with salt and cayenne pepper.
4 Cover the fish with sliced tomato, sprinkle with sugar and chopped parsley.
5 Simmer until the fish is cooked. Serve with creamed potatoes.

Herring and bacon

cooking time 8 10 minutes

you will need:

1 herring, trimmed and	fine oatmeal
filleted	1 rasher bacon
milk	bacon fat or margarine
salt and pepper	for frying

1 Dip the prepared herring in a little milk and then into fine oatmeal. Press the oatmeal on to the fish so that it is well coated and then shake gently to remove any loose oats.
2 Melt the bacon fat or margarine over a gentle heat.
3 Add the fish, flesh side down, and cook for about 4 minutes.
4 Turn over carefully and continue to cook.
5 Trim and grill the bacon.
6 Place the cooked herrings on a hot dish, top with a bacon rasher, and serve at once.

Baked stuffed herring

cooking time 20 minutes

you will need:

1 large herring (or medium sized mackerel)	1 heaped teaspoon breadcrumbs
$\frac{1}{4}$ cooking apple, finely chopped	1 teaspoon shredded suet
pinch sugar	squeeze lemon juice

1 Ask the fishmonger to gut the fish from the head, without cutting down the belly.
2 Rinse the fish, scraping off the scales, working from tail to head. Cut off the head.
3 Season the cavity with a little salt and pepper.
4 Mix the apple, breadcrumbs, suet, lemon juice, and sugar thoroughly.
5 Pack the stuffing into the fish and place in a buttered dish.
6 Cover with a piece of buttered paper and bake in a moderate oven (350° F.—Gas Mark 4).
7 Serve garnished with lemon slices and chopped parsley if liked.

Soused herrings

cooking time 40 minutes

you will need:

2 small herrings	$\frac{1}{2}$ level teaspoon mixed pickling spice
$\frac{1}{2}$ Spanish onion	
salt and pepper	vinegar
1 bay leaf	

1 Wash and scale the herrings. Cut off the heads.
2 Split the herrings open and remove the gut and backbone.
3 Place a slice of onion in the centre of each herring and roll the fish up, starting at the neck end.
4 Pack the fish closely together in a small pie dish. Sprinkle with salt and pepper and the pickling spice. Add the bay leaf.
5 Half fill the dish with equal quantities of vinegar and cold water.
6 Bake in a moderate oven (350° F.—Gas Mark 4).
7 Serve cold with salad or serve hot or cold with bread and butter.

Chicken meals for one

An individual chicken joint makes an easily cooked, tasty, and very nourishing meal for one person.

A chicken quarter usually weighs about 8 oz. and it may either be a wing and breast or a leg and thigh joint. If too large the latter may be divided in half again through the 'knee' joint.

All the chicken joints on sale today are from young and tender birds so it is quite safe to cook them by whatever method is most convenient. This may be frying or grilling or equally well, poaching, baking or casseroling. Sometimes it is useful to cook two joints at the same time to have chicken ready for a packed lunch or cold supper the next day.

For best flavour cook the joints within 12 hours of purchase. If frozen they need about 3-4 hours to thaw out at room temperature.

Chicken in mushroom cream sauce

cooking time about 35 minutes

you will need:

1 chicken quarter	$\frac{1}{2}$ can condensed mushroom soup
$\frac{1}{2}$ oz. butter	
1 teaspoon onion, finely chopped	4 tablespoons milk
$\frac{1}{4}$ teaspoon lemon juice	2 tablespoons cream

1 Heat the butter in a shallow pan without a lid. Fry the onion and the chicken joint slowly, uncovered, until the chicken begins to colour. Turn it from time to time.
2 Blend the soup and milk together. Pour it over the chicken.
3 Cover the pan and simmer gently for 20-30 minutes, stirring occasionally.
4 Remove lid, stir in cream and lemon juice and serve.

Grilled chicken with bacon

cooking time 25–30 minutes

you will need:

1 chicken quarter	2 teaspoons vegetable oil
½ lemon	1 rasher streaky bacon,
salt	chopped
1 oz. butter	2 oz. mushrooms, sliced

1 Rub the chicken joint over with cut lemon and sprinkle with salt.
2 Heat butter and oil in grill pan (rack removed) arranging pan in lowest position and at least 6 inches below heat.
3 Lay chicken skin side down in the pan and brush all over with melted fat.
4 Cook *slowly*, under medium to low heat, for 15 minutes.
5 Turn chicken, brush with fat, and add bacon and mushrooms to pan, turning them in the fat.
6 Continue cooking slowly for another 10–15 minutes, brushing chicken with fat from time to time, until cooked through and golden.
7 Dish the chicken. Add a squeeze of lemon juice to the pan and pour bacon, mushrooms and juices over the chicken.
8 Serve with potato crisps and watercress if liked.

Fried chicken with cream gravy

cooking time about 35 minutes

you will need:

1 chicken quarter	vegetable oil for frying
salt	*gravy:*
little milk	¼ pint top of milk
seasoned flour	¼ chicken stock cube

1 Rub the chicken joint with salt, dip in milk and then coat thoroughly with seasoned flour.
2 Pour sufficient oil into the frying pan to give a depth of ½ inch and heat gently until a drop of water hisses and sizzles in the fat.
3 Fry the chicken skin side down until browned, then reduce the heat and fry *slowly*, turning from time to time until cooked through, about 25–30 minutes in all, depending on the joint.
4 Drain and dish the chicken.
5 To make the cream gravy drain off all but 2 teaspoons of oil then work in a heaped teaspoon of the seasoned flour and stir for a minute or so.
6 Stir in the top of milk and cook until thickened, stirring all the time. If available add a quarter of a chicken stock cube dissolved in a tablespoon of water to the thickened sauce.

One pot chicken meal

cooking time about 40 minutes

you will need:

1 chicken quarter	2 large tomatoes, skinned
seasoned flour	and chopped
1 oz. butter or dripping	1 large potato, peeled and
1 tablespoon chopped	cut in ¼ inch dice
onion	chopped fresh herbs, if
	available

1 Coat the chicken with seasoned flour.
2 Heat the fat in a heavy saucepan and fry the onion over a gentle heat until it begins to soften.
3 Add the chicken, skin side downwards, and fry until golden.
4 Turn the chicken over, add the tomatoes, the diced potatoes and seasoning to taste.
5 Cover tightly and simmer over a low heat for 20–30 minutes until cooked. Sprinkle with herbs and serve.

Crunchy baked chicken (to eat hot or cold)

cooking time 40–45 minutes

you will need:

1 chicken quarter	little evaporated or
salt	top of milk
1 rounded tablespoon flour	1 small packet potato
	crisps

1 Rub chicken joint all over with salt then coat evenly with flour.
2 Crush the potato crisps with a rolling pin on a sheet of greaseproof paper.
3 Dip the chicken joint in milk, drain, then coat thickly and evenly with potato crisp crumbs.
4 Place skin side up on a baking sheet and cook in a moderate oven (350° F.—Gas Mark 4) until tender.
5 Serve hot with vegetables or cold with salad. Excellent for packed meals or picnics.

Chicken with savoury rice

cooking time 30 minutes

you will need:

1 chicken quarter	1½ oz. long grain rice
1 tablespoon olive oil	¼ pint chicken stock made
1 tablespoon chopped onion	from cube
1 small clove garlic	1 dessertspoon tomato
(optional)	purée
1 rasher streaky bacon,	salt and pepper
chopped	

Heat the oil in a heavy pan (with well fitting lid) and fry the chicken until golden on both sides, about 10 minutes.

Add the onion, crushed garlic and bacon and fry for 2-3 minutes. Then add in the rice and stir until rice changes colour.

Add the stock, tomato purée and seasoning to taste and bring to the boil.

4 Cover pan tightly then reduce heat and simmer gently for 15 minutes until rice and chicken are tender and liquid absorbed.

5 If liked a few cooked peas, strips of green pepper or slices of green olive may be added for the last 5 minutes of cooking.

Lunch and supper dishes

Creamy cheese soup

cooking time 10 minutes

you will need:

½ can condensed cream mushroom soup
½ soup can water
1 oz. grated Cheddar cheese
pinch black pepper

Stir cream of mushroom soup and water in a saucepan until smooth.

Blend in remaining ingredients.

Heat, stirring until cheese is melted.

Worcestershire sauce may be added to taste if liked. This can also be made with other soups (green pea, tomato, cream of asparagus, celery or chicken).

Vegetable soup with meat dumplings

cooking time 15–20 minutes

you will need:

2 oz. self-raising flour
pinch pepper
2 tablespoons water
good pinch salt
1 oz. shredded suet
2 oz. corned beef
1 can vegetable soup

Sift the flour, pepper, and salt together into a bowl. Add the suet.

Cut the corned beef into small dice and add to the flour.

Mix to a fairly firm dough with the water.

Using floured hands, form into 3–4 balls.

Bring the soup to the boil and add the dumplings.

Cover and cook gently.

Soup Italienne

cooking time 15 minutes

you will need:

2 oz. minced beef
½ oz. dripping
½ soup can water
½ can condensed minestrone soup

Shape meat into 3–4 small balls (if desired add a pinch of mixed herbs before shaping).

2 Brown slowly in melted fat in a saucepan.

3 Pour off any excess dripping. Stir in soup and water. Simmer for about 10 minutes.

Italian macaroni

cooking time about 20 minutes

you will need:

3 oz. macaroni
½ pint thick cheese sauce (see page 69)
3 tomatoes
salt and pepper
2 oz. grated cheddar cheese

1 Cook the macaroni in boiling salted water until tender.

2 Heat the sauce if necessary and add the skinned tomatoes cut in quarters.

3 Drain the macaroni, add to the sauce and season to taste.

4 Pour into a greased pie dish and sprinkle with cheese.

5 Place under a hot grill until golden brown.

Kedgeree with cheese

cooking time 10 minutes

you will need:

2 oz. cooked smoked haddock
1 hard-boiled egg
2 oz. cooked rice
½ oz. butter
salt and pinch cayenne pepper
1 oz. grated cheese
chopped parsley (optional)
½ lemon

1 Remove skin and bones from the fish while it is hot and flake the fish roughly.

2 Chop the egg white and yolk separately.

3 Mix the fish, egg white, cooked rice and seasoning in a saucepan.

4 Add butter and cook over a gentle heat for about 10 minutes.

5 Add the grated cheese and mix in quickly with a fork.

6 Pile the mixture on to a hot dish and garnish with chopped parsley if used, and the egg yolk. Serve at once with quarters of lemon.

Fish and cheese savoury

cooking time 30 minutes

you will need:

3 oz. smoked haddock	salt and pepper
½ pint white sauce (see	2 slices bread
page 68)	2 tomatoes
2 teaspoons capers	2 oz. cheese
little sugar	

1 Sprinkle the fish with salt and pepper and steam between two plates.
2 When cooked, flake and leave in a bowl.
3 Make the white sauce, add the capers and leave in a bowl or jug covered with grease-proof paper that has been dampened with cold water.
4 To serve, halve the tomatoes, sprinkle with sugar, salt and pepper. Grill until brown.
5 Toast the bread, add the fish to the sauce, heat gently.
6 Meanwhile cut the cheese into triangles or slices and when the fish is heated through, pour into a heatproof dish and cover with the cheese.
7 Place under the grill until golden brown and the cheese is bubbling.
8 Serve with tomatoes and toast. Makes sufficient for 2 servings.

Surprise potato

cooking time about 1 hour 15 minutes

you will need:

1 large potato	salt and pepper
1 egg	nutmeg
butter	

1 Scrub potato, rinse and dry well.
2 Rub with butter, prick with a fork, bake in a moderately hot oven (375° F.—Gas Mark 5) for about 1 hour until soft.
3 Cut off top lengthways. Scoop inside out carefully. Mash with salt, pepper, butter and nutmeg to taste.
4 Half fill skin, break an egg into the skin and season.
5 Dot with butter and replace in a moderate oven (350° F.—Gas Mark 4) for about 15 minutes until the egg is set.
6 A little chopped fried onion, tomato or bacon or a spoonful of cooked vegetables may be put into the skin before the egg is added.

Surprise tomatoes

cooking time 30 minutes

you will need:

1 large tomato	butter or margarine
salt and pepper	½–1 oz. grated cheese
1 egg	

1 Remove the stalk from the tomato and make a circular cut in the stalk end. Scoop out the seeds and juice, leaving some tomato flesh in the tomato.
2 Sprinkle the inside with salt and pepper and break the egg into the tomato. Dot with butter and sprinkle with cheese.
3 Bake in a moderate oven, 350° F.—Gas Mark 4, until the egg is set.

Egg and sausageburger

cooking time 20 minutes

you will need:

2 oz. pork sausage meat	1 bap
½ oz. fat	salt and pepper
1 egg	tomato sauce or chutney

1 Shape the sausage meat into a thin flat cake, using lightly floured hands.
2 Fry in hot fat until golden brown on both sides, drain and keep hot.
3 Fry the egg in the remaining fat in the pan, spooning the hot fat over the top of the egg to cook the yolk thoroughly.
4 Cut the bap in half and toast the inside.
5 Spread the bottom half of the bap with a little sauce or chutney, top with the round of sausage meat and the egg.
6 Season with salt and pepper, cover with the top half of the bap. Serve at once.
Sliced fried onions may be used instead of the tomato sauce, and the burger may be topped with a slice of cheese and grilled.

Fish cakes

cooking time 10 minutes

you will need:

4 oz. cooked white fish	4 oz. mashed potatoes
½ egg	1 teaspoon chopped
few drops lemon juice	parsley
	salt and pepper

1 Flake fish, mix with potato and parsley. Season to taste.
2 Add lemon juice, bind mixture with egg.
3 Divide into 2 or 3 portions. Shape into cakes.
4 Fry in hot butter or bacon dripping until brown on each side.
5 Fish cakes may be dipped in egg and breadcrumbs before frying. They may also be grilled (see page 12).

Savoury cutlets

cooking time 3–4 minutes each

you will need:

4 oz. cooked meat or fish	½ teaspoon chopped
4 tablespoons thick white	parsley (optional)
sauce (see page 68)	flour
salt and pepper	egg
½ teaspoon made mustard	browned crumbs
	fat for frying

1 Finely chop the meat or fish.
2 Mix with the sauce, seasoning and parsley—if used.
3 Spread the mixture on a plate and leave in a cool place until firm.
4 Turn out on to a floured surface, divide into equal proportions and shape into cutlets.
5 Dip in flour, then in egg and breadcrumbs.
6 Fry in deep fat until golden brown.
7 Drain well and serve with tomato sauce.
2 oz. ham and 1 hard-boiled egg may be used instead of meat.

Baked beans and bacon

cooking time about 10 minutes

you will need:

1 rasher streaky bacon	salt and pepper
1 teaspoon bacon dripping	good pinch sugar
or butter	(optional)
1 small can baked beans	1 large slice bread
1 teaspoon tomato sauce	1 dessertspoon bacon
(optional)	dripping

1 Chop the bacon, removing rind.
2 Fry in a saucepan over a moderate heat until crisp.
3 Add 1 teaspoon fat and stir over a low heat until melted.
4 Add the beans and tomato sauce if used. Mix well, season to taste and add the sugar if used.
5 Cover and heat gently, stirring occasionally.
6 Meanwhile fry the bread in the remaining fat until crisp and golden on both sides.
7 Top with beans and bacon and serve at once.

Variations

Serve the beans and bacon on hot toast spread with butter.
Serve with diced, left-over potatoes, fried until golden brown in place of the bread.
Instead of bacon, any of the following could be used: diced or chopped canned or cooked meat, skinned and diced breakfast or continental sausage, diced kidneys or liver.
Serve with poached or fried eggs or grilled or baked tomatoes.

Curried beans and potato cake

cooking time 20–30 minutes

you will need:

4 oz. potatoes	about 1 oz. flour
good pinch salt	½ oz. dripping
½ oz. butter or margarine	1 small can curried beans

1 Boil the potatoes, drain and sieve, add the salt, butter or margarine. Work in as much flour as the potato will easily absorb.
2 Turn on to a floured board and knead lightly.
3 Roll out to ½ inch thickness and cut into 2 rounds.
4 Heat the dripping and fry the potato cakes on both sides for about 8 minutes.
5 Place on a serving dish and keep hot.
6 Heat the beans through and pile on top of the potato cakes and serve.
7 If liked a little grated cheese or finely chopped onion can be added to the potato.
If you cook extra potatoes to use later as potato cakes, make the cakes while the potatoes are still warm and fry when required.

Welsh rarebit

cooking time 3–4 minutes

you will need:

3 oz. grated cheese	1 egg yolk
1 teaspoon made mustard	1 tablespoon milk
salt and cayenne pepper	1 tablespoon melted
1 round hot toast	butter or margarine

1 Mix all ingredients together in a bowl and spread evenly on the toast.
2 Place under a hot grill and cook for a few minutes until golden brown.
3 Serve immediately.

Mushroom savoury

cooking time 20–30 minutes

you will need:

2 flat mushrooms	1 round toast
½ rasher bacon	1 oz. butter
2 pieces soft herring roe	salt and pepper

1 Trim, rinse and dry mushrooms, brush with butter and grill.
2 If using fresh herring roes, lightly flour and cook in melted butter in saucepan.
Canned herring roes can be heated through with a nut of butter in the grill pan.
3 Make the toast and grill the bacon.
4 Lay the bacon on the toast, cover with herring roes and top with mushrooms.
5 Season with pepper and salt.

Spaghetti with mushrooms and bacon

cooking time about 25 minutes

you will need:

3 oz. spaghetti	1 tablespoon tomato
2 oz. mushrooms	purée
2 oz. bacon	2–3 tablespoons stock
½ oz. butter	salt and pepper
	grated cheese (optional)

1 Cook the spaghetti in plenty of boiling salted water for 20 minutes or until tender. Drain well and put on a hot serving dish.
2 Chop the mushrooms and bacon and cook in the butter until tender.
3 Stir in the tomato purée and stock, add seasoning to taste.
4 Pile on top of the spaghetti. Sprinkle with grated cheese and serve.

Cheese and onion pasty

cooking time 20–30 minutes

you will need:

4 oz. short crust pastry	salt, pepper and nutmeg
(see page 67)	1 egg
1 large onion	2–3 oz. grated cheese
½ oz. flour	¼ pint milk

1 Line a small deep pie plate with half the pastry.
2 Slice the onion.
3 Add the seasoning to the flour and toss the onion in this.
4 Beat the egg and stir in the milk and cheese.
5 Place the onion in the pastry case and pour the cheese mixture over.
6 Cover with remaining pastry, seal and flute the edges.
7 Make a hole in the centre of the lid for the steam to escape.
8 Bake in a hot oven (400° F.—Gas mark 6).
Sliced mushrooms or eating apple may be used in place of onion, and chopped cooked bacon or ham may be added.

Stuffed tomatoes

cooking time 15 minutes

you will need:

2 large tomatoes	2 heaped tablespoons
pinch salt and pepper	cooked rice or sweet
pinch sugar	corn
½ oz. butter	2 rashers bacon

1 Cut the top off each tomato, remove the pulp with a small spoon.
2 Sprinkle the inside of each tomato with salt, pepper and sugar.

3 Remove rind from bacon, chop roughly and fry for 5 minutes. Remove from pan and drain.
4 Mix bacon with rice or sweet corn and tomato pulp.
5 Fill tomatoes with bacon mixture, dot each with butter.
6 Bake in a moderate oven (350° F.—Gas Mark 4) or grill until heated through, about 10 minutes.
Alternatively omit butter and top each tomato with a tablespoon of cheese sauce.

Savoury fritters

cooking time 3–4 minutes each

you will need:

French batter (see page 68)	1 oz. seasoned flour
3–4 slices pork luncheon	apple sauce or chutney
meat	

1 Make French batter.
2 Toss slices of meat in flour.
3 Dip into batter using a fork or skewer, allow surplus batter to drip off.
4 Fry in hot fat for 3–4 minutes.
5 Drain on crumpled kitchen paper.
6 Serve very hot accompanied by apple sauce or chutney.
Peeled sliced potatoes, apples and oranges or whole bananas may be cooked in the same way. Omit seasoning from flour when making fruit fritters and serve dusted with castor sugar.

Individual toad-in-the-hole

cooking time 40–50 minutes

you will need:

2 oz. plain flour	little milk
pinch salt and pepper	4 pork sausages
1 egg	little cooking fat

1 Melt the fat in an ovenproof dish in a hot oven (400° F.—Gas Mark 6).
2 Add the pricked sausages and cook in the oven for about 10 minutes, turning once.
3 Sieve the flour, salt and pepper into a bowl. Make a well in the centre and add the egg.
4 Beat until smooth, adding enough milk to make a fairly thick batter.
5 When the sausages are lightly browned, pour the batter over them and cook for about 30–40 minutes until the batter is well risen, crisp and brown. Serve at once.
If liked, a pinch of dried mixed herbs may be added to the batter.

Sweet corn fritters

cooking time 2–3 minutes each

you will need:

French batter (see page 68)   1 teaspoon finely chopped
2 heaped tablespoons   onion
    sweet corn   fat for frying

1 Make French batter.
2 Stir in drained sweet corn and onion.
3 Drop tablespoons of mixture into hot fat.
4 Fry until golden brown on both sides.
5 Drain and serve as an accompaniment to cold meat, fried bacon or fried chicken or sprinkled with grated cheese as a supper snack.

Savoury stuffed pancakes

cooking time 35 minutes

you will need:

1 small grated onion   salt and pepper
¼ pint pancake batter (see   ¼ pint thin cheese sauce
    page 68)   (see page 69)
4–6 oz. minced cooked   1 oz. grated cheese
    vegetables, meat or fish

1 Stir the onion into the pancake batter.
2 Fry the pancakes and keep them warm.
3 Season the filling ingredients to taste.
4 Place an equal quantity on each pancake and roll it up.
5 Arrange the pancakes in an ovenproof dish, pour on the cheese sauce and sprinkle with grated cheese.
6 Bake in a hot oven (400° F.—Gas Mark 6) for 15 minutes.

Corned beef on toast

cooking time 20–30 minutes

you will need:

½ oz. butter or margarine   pinch salt
1 teaspoon finely chopped   pinch curry powder
    onion   1 teaspoon Worcestershire
½ level tablespoon flour   sauce
4 tablespoons water   4 oz. corned beef
½ beef extract cube   2 slices toast

1 Chop the corned beef.
2 Melt the butter or margarine in a small pan, add the onion and cook until soft.
3 Stir in the flour and cook for a further 2 3 minutes.
4 Add the water and crumble in the beef cube.
5 Add the salt, curry powder and Worcestershire sauce. Stir until the sauce boils and thickens. Reduce heat.
6 Add the corned beef and allow to heat through.
7 Serve on toast.

Savoury egg special

cooking time 15 minutes

you will need:

1 slice bread   1 slice processed cheese
½ oz. butter   1 egg
1 slice canned tongue or   1 small packet frozen
    ham   spinach

1 Cook spinach according to directions on packet.
2 Poach egg, toast bread and spread with butter.
3 Cover toast with tongue or ham and top with cheese.
4 Cook under grill until cheese melts. Place poached egg on top.
5 Serve immediately with drained spinach.

Bacon and banana savoury

cooking time 10–15 minutes

you will need:

1 banana   ¼ pint cheese sauce (see
2 rashers bacon   page 69) or thin slice
1 slice bread   cheese
¼ oz. butter (optional) or
    little made mustard

1 Cut banana in half lengthways.
2 Wrap each half in a bacon rasher.
3 Toast bread on one side. Spread untoasted side with butter or smear lightly with mustard.
4 Place bananas on untoasted side of bread and grill until bacon is cooked. Turn once or twice during cooking so that bacon is thoroughly cooked.
5 Top with cheese sauce or thin slice of cheese when the bacon is cooked. Brown under grill and serve at once.

Toasted supper sandwich

cooking time about 6 minutes

you will need:

2 slices toast   1 pineapple ring
1 slice ham or cooked   ¼ pint thick cheese sauce
    bacon   (see page 69)

1 Place slice of ham on one slice of toast.
2 Top ham with pineapple ring and pour cheese sauce over.
3 Cook under hot grill until golden.
4 Top with second slice of toast, cut through diagonally. Serve at once.

Variation

Apple rings may be used instead of pineapple. Peel and core 1 cooking apple, dust with sugar, dot with butter or bacon fat. Fry or grill until tender, about 5 minutes. Apple rings also make an excellent accompaniment to fried or grilled bacon or herrings.

French toasted sandwich

cooking time 10 minutes

you will need:

1 slice ham or luncheon meat	½ egg
1 teaspoon chutney	2 tablespoons milk
good pinch salt and pepper	pinch sugar and salt
2 thin slices sandwich loaf	sprinkle of pepper
	butter or margarine

1 Make a sandwich with unbuttered bread, meat and chutney.
2 Mix the egg, milk, sugar and seasoning together. Dip sandwich into the egg mixture, coating on both sides.
3 Melt the butter or margarine in a frying pan and gently fry the sandwich on both sides until golden brown.
4 Serve hot with extra chutney, fried apple rings or a sliced tomato.
Cheese may be used in place of meat.

Double decker toasted sandwich

cooking time 6 minutes

you will need:

2 slices bread	1 slice cheese
butter	1 large tomato
2 slices corned beef or minced beef loaf	

1 Toast the bread on one side.
2 Butter the untoasted side of the bread. Cover 1 slice with meat, 1 with cheese.
3 Grill both until the meat sizzles and the cheese is slightly browned.
4 Sandwich together with cheese on top.
5 Cut through diagonally, serve with a grilled tomato.

Cinnamon toast

you will need:

2 slices hot toast, spread with butter	2 heaped teaspoons castor or brown sugar, or to
¼ teaspoon ground cinnamon	taste

1 Mix the cinnamon and sugar together thoroughly.
2 Sprinkle the hot toast with the mixture and place under a hot grill for about ½ minute. Serve very hot with fruit.

Savoury oven toast

cooking time 20–30 minutes

you will need:

2 slices of thickly buttered bread, ¼ inch thick	meat or fish paste anchovy paste
one of the following:	grated cheese
meat or vegetable extract	salt and pepper – if liked

1 Cut the crusts off the slices of bread.
2 Spread with any of the spreads mentioned above.
3 Season if liked and place on a baking tray.
4 Toast in hot oven (400° F.—Gas Mark 6) on the second shelf from the top.
5 Cut into fingers and serve very hot with soup.

Meat and vegetable pie

cooking time about 45 minutes

you will need:

4 oz. cooked or canned meat	1 oz. flour
2 tablespoons table sauce or chutney	2 carrots
	2 celery sticks
½ pint stock or water	salt and pepper
2 onions	8 oz. cooked mashed potato
1 oz. dripping	

1 Slice carrots, chop celery and cook in boiling salted water until tender. Drain, saving the liquid.
2 Chop the onions, fry in the dripping until soft.
3 Blend in the flour, cook for three minutes.
4 Gradually stir in the liquid, use water in which the vegetables were cooked made up to ½ pint if necessary.
5 Bring to the boil, stirring, allow to boil for 3 minutes, add the chutney and salt and pepper to taste.
6 Cut the meat into cubes, mix with the vegetables and place in a greased pie dish.
7 Pour the gravy over and cover with mashed potato.
8 Smooth the potato and mark with the back of a fork.
9 Brush with milk or beaten egg. Bake in a moderately hot oven (375° F.—Gas Mark 5) for 30 minutes.
Sufficient for two servings.

Savoury meat cakes

cooking time about 20 minutes

you will need:

4 oz. cooked or canned meat	1 teaspoon meat extract
1 small onion	½ teaspoon table sauce
½ oz. dripping	seasoning
1 heaped dessertspoon flour	beaten egg or milk
4–5 tablespoons stock or water	browned breadcrumbs
	fat for frying

1 Mince or chop the meat finely.
2 Chop the onion and fry in the dripping until soft.
3 Blend in the flour, cook for three minutes over a gentle heat.

4 Stir in the liquid, gradually. Cook until the mixture thickens, stirring throughout.

5 Add the meat extract, sauce and salt and pepper to taste.

6 Stir in the meat, remove pan from heat and leave until mixture is cool enough to handle.

7 Shape into two flat cakes, with floured hands.

8 Brush with beaten egg or milk and coat with breadcrumbs.

9 Fry in hot fat until brown on both sides.

10 Drain and serve hot with tomato sauce and vegetables or cold with salad and mixed pickles.

Savoury rice with sausages

cooking time 30–40 minutes

you will need:

2 oz. rice	2 or 3 pork sausages
½ oz. margarine	½ oz. dripping
1 small onion	Worcestershire sauce
bare ½ pint tomato soup	(optional)
salt and pepper	sugar (optional)

1 Chop the onion and cook in melted margarine until soft, but not coloured.

2 Add the rice, continue to cook gently for two or three minutes, stirring throughout.

3 Stir in the tomato soup, which may be seasoned to taste with sugar and sauce if liked.

4 Bring to the boil, stirring.

5 Reduce heat, cover and cook over a gentle heat until the rice is cooked and the liquid absorbed.

6 Meanwhile fry the sausages in dripping, over a gentle heat.

7 Tip the rice into a warm dish, drain the sausages, cut them through lengthwise if liked. Pile sausages on rice and serve at once.

Chopped cooked ham or bacon may be added to the rice during the last 10 minutes of cooking. Omit sausages but serve with a fried egg if liked.

Pork chops with apple

cooking time 15–20 minutes

you will need:

1 pork chop	½ oz. butter
1 small green apple	1 teaspoon sugar

1 Brush the chops with oil or melted butter and grill under a medium grill turning at 5 minute intervals.

2 Meanwhile, peel and core the apple, cut into thick slices and fry quickly in melted butter until lightly browned. Sprinkle with sugar and fry until the edges of the apple are crisp.

3 Serve the fried apple with the chops.

Mint chops

cooking time 15–20 minutes

you will need:

1 lamb chop	½ oz. butter
1 teaspoon chopped parsley	grilled tomatoes
1 teaspoon chopped mint	

1 Cut a slit 2 inches long in the chop from the outer edge to the bone, to form a 'pocket'.

2 Beat the parsley, mint and butter together and stuff into the pocket.

3 Grill the chop until tender and serve with grilled tomatoes.

Steak with parsley and onion butter

cooking time 15–20 minutes

you will need:

2 spring onions	1 teaspoon chopped
1 oz. butter	chervil or tarragon
1 teaspoon finely chopped parsley	1 entrecote steak

1 Chop the onions very finely and mix with the melted butter, parsley and chervil or tarragon. Keep hot.

2 Grill the steak to tenderness liked and toss in the sauce. Serve at once.

Cheese steak

cooking time 15–20 minutes

you will need:

¼ clove garlic	1 fillet steak, cut 1 inch
1½ oz. Cheshire cheese	thick

1 Crush the garlic and mix with the crumbled cheese.

2 Grill the steak on one side until brown.

3 Turn the steak over and spread with the cheese mixture.

4 Continue to grill until the cheese is melted and the meat cooked.

Pork chops rosemary

cooking time 30 minutes

you will need:

2 pork chops, cut ½–1 inch thick	1 8-oz. can whole peeled tomatoes
little fat	pinch rosemary

1 Trim off the surplus fat from the chops.

2 Heat the fat and brown the chops quickly on both sides.

3 Mix the rosemary with the tomatoes.

4 Place the chops in a casserole, pour the tomatoes over, cover and bake in a moderately hot oven 375° F.– Gas Mark 5.

5 Serve with baked potatoes. This is enough for 2 servings.

American beef hash

cooking time 25 minutes

you will need:

4 oz. cold, cooked beef	1–2 tablespoons thick
4 oz. cold cooked potatoes	gravy
salt and pepper	tomato ketchup
1 oz. butter or margarine	mushroom ketchup
parsley	

1 Cut the meat and potatoes into cubes.
2 Season the potatoes with salt and pepper.
3 Toss in a little butter or margarine.
4 Place half the potatoes and the meat in a saucepan and bind with the gravy, flavoured with tomato and mushroom ketchup.
5 Heat gently together until thoroughly hot.
6 Meanwhile, fry the remaining potatoes until crisp and brown.
7 Turn the meat mixture on to a hot plate, top with the fried potatoes, sprinkle with parsley and serve at once.

Salmon patties

cooking time about 20 minutes

you will need:

1 small can salmon	1 tablespoon tomato sauce
½ oz. margarine	1 heaped teaspoon
1 heaped dessertspoon	chopped parsley
flour	seasoning
5 tablespoons liquid from	milk or beaten egg
can made up with milk	browned breadcrumbs
2 teaspoons vinegar	fat for frying

1 Drain the salmon (saving the liquid) mash with a fork, removing bones.
2 Melt the margarine, blend in the flour and cook over a gentle heat for 3 minutes.
3 Stir in the liquid gradually, bring to the boil, boil for 2–3 minutes, stirring.
4 Remove from heat, stir in vinegar, tomato sauce and parsley. Add fish and seasoning to taste.
5 Leave until cool, form into two rounds, with floured hands.
6 Brush with milk or egg and coat with breadcrumbs.
7 Fry in hot fat until golden on both sides.
8 Drain and serve with parsley sauce if liked.

Meat balls

cooking time 30 minutes

you will need:

4 oz. raw minced beef	lemon rind
2 oz. breadcrumbs	seasoning
1 dessertspoon chopped	nutmeg
parsley	1 egg
1 small onion, finely	
chopped	

1 Mix the meat, breadcrumbs, parsley, onion, lemon rind, salt and pepper to taste and a sprinkle of grated nutmeg together in a bowl.
2 Bind with the beaten egg.
3 Form into small balls and cook in boiling salted water for 20–30 minutes.

Halibut with almond sauce

cooking time 10–15 minutes

you will need:

1 halibut steak	sauce:
oil or butter	1 oz. blanched almonds
salt and pepper	¼ oz. butter
lemon juice	⅛ pint cream or top of milk

1 Brush the halibut with oil or melted butter.
2 Sprinkle with salt and pepper and lemon juice.
3 Grill for 4–5 minutes on each side.
4 Meanwhile, make the sauce by browning the almonds in the butter and add the cream. Heat, but do not boil.
5 Serve with the halibut.

Cod fillet au gratin

cooking time 10–15 minutes

you will need:

1 small packet frozen	¼ pint cheese sauce
broccoli	(see page 69)
4–6 oz. cod fillet	salt and pepper
little oil	1 oz. grated cheese

1 Cook the broccoli according to the directions on the packet until just tender.
2 Brush the cod fillets with oil and grill for 5 minutes on each side.
3 Place the broccoli in a hot dish. Arrange the fish on top, cover with the cheese sauce.
4 Sprinkle the grated cheese on top and brown. Serve at once with fingers of toast.

Sole with sour cream sauce

cooking time about 10 minutes

you will need:

1 small sole	¼ oz. butter
melted butter	1 tablespoon chopped
sauce:	parsley
2 small tomatoes	½ jar or carton yoghourt
¼ clove garlic	

1 Make the sauce by frying the tomatoes and garlic in the butter. Add the parsley and yoghourt just before serving.
2 Wash the sole and remove the black skin.
3 Brush the sole with melted butter and cook under a hot grill for 2–3 minutes on each side.
4 Serve the sole with sauce poured over it.

Curried cod

cooking time 35–40 minutes

you will need:

½ small packet frozen cod	1 hard-boiled egg
1 oz. butter	½ teaspoon chopped
½ teaspoon curry powder	parsley
½ tablespoon flour	

Cut the cod into slices and place in a greased ovenproof dish.

Melt the butter, add the curry powder and cook for about 10 minutes, stirring occasionally. Blend in the flour and cook for 2 minutes. Pour this mixture over the fish.

Cook in a hot oven (425° F.—Gas Mark 7) for 25 minutes.

When cooked, sprinkle with hot chopped hard-boiled egg and parsley and serve at once.

Eastern fish steak

cooking time 20–30 minutes

you will need:

1 oz. blanched almonds	1 cod steak
1 oz. seedless raisins	1 tablespoon flour
2 oz. butter	

Fry the almonds and raisins in 1 oz. butter until just golden brown. Drain carefully and keep hot.

Wash, trim and dry the fish and coat with flour.

Melt remaining butter in a frying pan, add the steak, cover, and cook slowly on both sides until done.

Put the fish into a dish with the almonds and raisins. Serve with broccoli.

Curried fish cakes

cooking time 20–30 minutes

you will need:

8 oz. cod's roe, cooked	1 egg
and chopped	breadcrumbs
2 tablespoons cold boiled	fat for frying
Patna rice	
curry sauce (see page 70)	

Mix the fish and rice together and moisten with curry sauce.

Shape into small balls and coat with egg and breadcrumbs.

Fry until golden brown.

Serve accompanied by curry sauce.

Tuna cutlets

cooking time 20–30 minutes

you will need:

½ pint white sauce	breadcrumbs
(see page 68)	parsley
anchovy essence	tomato sauce
1 egg	
3 oz. canned tuna	

1 Flake the tuna and add it with the beaten egg to the white sauce. Add anchovy essence to taste and heat through very gently.

2 Spread the mixture on a cold plate and leave to become cold.

3 When cold, cut into cutlet shapes and coat each with egg and breadcrumbs. Fry in deep fat until golden brown. Serve sprinkled with parsley.

Lunch time quickie

cooking time about 10 minutes

you will need:

1 slice bread	1 hard-boiled egg
chutney (optional)	1 large tomato
2 oz. liver sausage	salt, pepper and sugar

1 Toast bread on one side only.

2 Spread untoasted side with chutney if liked.

3 Cut liver sausages in slices, removing skin.

4 Place liver sausage on chutney and spread on toast.

5 Grill the liver sausage for 4–5 minutes.

6 Cover with slices of hard-boiled egg, sprinkle with salt and pepper.

7 Place slices of tomato on top of the egg, sprinkle with salt, pepper and sugar.

8 Grill for 3–4 minutes. Serve at once.
The liver sausage may be covered with scrambled egg, instead of hard-boiled egg. Serve with thin slices raw tomato.

Celery and bacon toast

cooking time about 15 minutes

you will need:

2 sticks celery	2 rashers bacon
1 dessertspoon grated	2 slices bread
cheese	

1 Chop celery and cook in boiling salted water until tender. Drain well.

2 Toast each slice of bread on one side only.

3 Place celery on one slice of bread, on the untoasted side, sprinkle with grated cheese.

4 Remove rind from bacon, cut rashers in half if necessary, place on untoasted side of second slice of bread.

5 Place under a hot grill until cheese is browned and bacon is cooked.

6 Put sandwich together, bacon side down on celery and cheese.

7 Cut through diagonally and serve.
Stewed unsweetened apple or mushrooms sautéed in butter may be used in place of celery.

Creamed rarebit

cooking time about 5 minutes

you will need:

1 oz. grated Cheddar cheese
1 dessertspoon salad cream
1 slice toast
½ teaspoon grated onion
or a few sultanas

1 Blend the cheese and salad cream.
2 Add the onion or sultanas.
3 Spread on toast and brown under a hot grill.
4 Serve at once, topped with a poached egg or grilled bacon if liked.

Pineapple toast special

cooking time 10 minutes

you will need:

1 slice toast
1 slice cooked ham
1 oz. grated Cheddar cheese
¾ teaspoon made mustard
seasoning
2–3 teaspoons milk
1 pineapple ring

1 Place slice of ham on toast.
2 Blend cheese, mustard and milk to a smooth paste adding salt and pepper to taste.
3 Spread cheese mixture over ham, grill until golden.
4 Top with pineapple ring, well drained, grill for 2–3 minutes longer, to heat pineapple ring.

Tuna toast

cooking time 15 minutes

you will need:

1 egg
1 teaspoon milk
good ½ oz. butter
2 oz. tuna fish
seasoning
1 slice buttered toast

1 Beat the egg adding the milk.
2 Melt the butter, add the tuna fish, drained and flaked.
3 Heat through for about 5 minutes, over a gentle heat.
4 Stir in the egg mixture, continue cooking until mixture is thick and creamy, stirring throughout with a fork.
5 Season to taste, pile on hot buttered toast.
1 teaspoon finely chopped onion may be cooked in the butter, before the fish is added, if liked

Herring roes and cheese on toast

cooking time 10 minutes

you will need:

4 oz. herring roes
1 oz. seasoned flour
2 oz. butter
1 slice toast
¼ pint cheese sauce (see page 69)

1 Wash the roes in salted water, drain, toss in seasoned flour.
2 Fry roes gently in melted butter for about 5 minutes.
3 Drain well, pile on toast, pour over the cheese sauce and cook under a hot grill until golden brown.

Swedish toast

cooking time 15 minutes

you will need:

1 egg
½ onion
½ oz. butter
1 or 2 anchovy fillets
1 slice toast

1 Hard boil the egg and chop it finely.
2 Chop or grate the onion, fry in butter until golden.
3 Chop the anchovy, add with the egg, to the cooked onion.
4 Continue cooking, for 2 or 3 minutes longer, stirring lightly.
5 Pile on toast and serve at once.

Fish supper savoury

cooking time 20 minutes

you will need:

2 fillets white fish
1 small onion
2–3 tablespoons chopped parsley
1 tablespoon chopped green pepper (optional)
½ small can tomato soup
salt and pepper

1 Cut the fillets in half, place in a small greased ovenproof dish. Sprinkle fish with salt and pepper.
2 Grate or finely chop the onion.
3 Mix onion, parsley and pepper if used. Sprinkle over fish.
4 Pour the tomato soup into the casserole, adding salt and pepper to taste.
5 Cover and bake in a moderate oven (350° F.—Gas Mark 4) until the vegetables and fish are tender.
6 Serve with rice or sweet corn niblets.

Sandwich snack

cooking time 15 minutes

you will need:

1 rasher bacon
1 tomato
salt, pepper and sugar
2 oz. mushrooms
3 slices bread
butter

1 Remove rind from bacon, chop roughly, fry for 2–3 minutes, until cooked but not crisp.

2 Remove bacon from pan, place on a warm plate and keep hot.

3 Slice tomato, sprinkle with salt, pepper and sugar, fry in bacon drippings for about 2 minutes. Remove from pan, keep hot.

4 Chop mushrooms and fry, adding a little more bacon drippings or butter to the pan.

5 Meanwhile toast bread, on one side only. Spread untoasted side of each slice with butter.

6 To serve, cover one buttered side of toast with bacon and tomato, the second with mushrooms.

7 Place the bacon and tomato slice on a warm plate, cover with mushroom slice and top with plain slice, buttered side down.

8 Cut through diagonally and serve at once accompanied with cheese sauce (see page 69), if liked.

Bacon grill

cooking time about 10 minutes

you will need:

1 back rasher, cut 1 inch thick	1 small apple
2–3 mushrooms	2–3 chipolata sausages
2 tomatoes	oil

1 Remove the rind from the bacon. Peel the mushrooms, halve the tomatoes, core and slice the apples, prick the sausages.

2 Grill the sausages and when nearly cooked, brush the mushrooms with oil and grill these.

3 Add the tomatoes and bacon and grill the apple rings for about 2 minutes on each side.

4 Serve with a green salad.

Barbecued ham slices

cooking time 15–20 minutes

you will need:

½ oz. brown sugar	1 gammon rasher
¼ tablespoon prepared mustard	boiled Patna rice
½ tablespoon vinegar	chopped pineapple
1 tablespoon pineapple juice	

1 Place the sugar, mustard, vinegar and pineapple juice in a small pan and simmer gently together for 5 minutes.

2 Brush the rasher with this mixture and grill for 10–15 minutes, turning and basting once.

3 Serve with boiled rice mixed with drained chopped pineapple.

Cheese and tomato dreams

cooking time 5–10 minutes

you will need:

2 large slices bread	tomato chutney
2 thin slices cheese	fat for frying
butter	

1 Butter the slices of bread on one side.

2 Spread each slice with tomato chutney and then place the slices of cheese on one piece of bread.

3 Sandwich firmly with the other slice of bread.

4 Fry until golden brown, cut in half and serve garnished with watercress.

Ham crôutes

cooking time 10 minutes

you will need:

2–3 rounds of bread (about 2 inches in diameter)	2 oz. ham, finely chopped
fat for frying	2 thin slices cheese
2–3 tablespoons white sauce (see page 68)	2–3 small gherkins (optional)

1 Fry the rounds of bread until crisp and golden and keep hot.

2 Add the ham to the white sauce, heat through and pile on to the rounds of fried bread.

3 Place a slice of cheese on top of each, place under a grill until the cheese is soft.

4 Garnish each with a small gherkin if liked.

Cheese and anchovy slices

cooking time 5–10 minutes

you will need:

1 large slice of bread	3 thin slices of cheese
butter	2 anchovy fillets

1 Lightly toast the bread on both sides, spread one side with butter.

2 Arrange the cheese slices, overlapping, on the buttered side.

3 Place under a hot grill until golden brown.

4 Garnish with the anchovy fillets.

Cheese toasties

cooking time 5–10 minutes

you will need:

1 large slice of bread	mustard
butter	Worcestershire sauce
2 thin slices of cheese	1 tomato

1 Toast the bread on one side only and butter the untoasted side.

2 Lightly smear the slices of cheese on one side, place on the toast and sprinkle lightly with a few drops of Worcestershire sauce.

3 Place under the grill until the cheese is soft and golden brown.

4 Garnish with slices of tomato and serve at once.

Cheese and apple on toast

cooking time about 10 minutes

you will need:

1 eating apple	milk
2 oz. grated cheese	buttered toast
1 teaspoon flour	parsley to garnish
salt and pepper	

1 Peel, core and dice the apple.
2 Mix with the cheese, flour, salt and pepper to taste and enough milk to bind.
3 Spread on to the toast and grill until golden brown. Garnish with parsley.

Roes on toast

cooking time about 10 minutes

you will need:

4 oz. herring roes	butter
1 tablespoon porridge oats	buttered toast
salt and pepper	

1 Wash the roes in salted water, drain and toss in porridge oats.
2 Place the roes on a greased grid, dot with butter and grill slowly for 5 minutes. Turn over, dot with butter and continue grilling for 4 5 minutes.
3 Serve at once on the buttered toast.

Sardine toasts

cooking time about 5 minutes

you will need:

½ can sardines	1 hard-boiled egg, chopped
2 tablespoons melted	salt and pepper
butter	1 tomato, sliced
1 oz. breadcrumbs	buttered toast

1 Drain the sardines and mash them.
2 Add the breadcrumbs to the butter and heat through in a saucepan.
3 Add the egg, sardines and salt and pepper to taste.
4 Pile on to buttered toast and grill until golden brown.
5 Garnish with slices of tomato and serve at once.

Cheese and meat club sandwich

cooking time 20 minutes

you will need:

3 slices buttered toast	1 slice cheese
2 lettuce leaves	1 large tomato
1 slice cooked meat	mayonnaise
chutney	seasoning

1 Top one slice of toast with lettuce, meat and a dab of chutney.
2 Cover with second slice of toast, top this with lettuce, cheese and tomato, cut into slices.
3 Sprinkle tomato with a little salt, pepper and sugar, spoon a little mayonnaise over.
4 Cover with third slice of toast and cut through diagonally. Serve while toast is still hot.
Club sandwich may be made with chicken in the bottom layer, and grilled bacon rasher in the top layer. Or with cooked fish instead of meat and hard boiled or scrambled egg replacing the cheese.

Hot decker sandwiches

Butter three slices hot brown toast. Cover one piece with scrambled egg to which a little chopped cheese has been added. Cover with the second slice of toast. Spread this piece with rashers of fried bacon and sprigs of watercress. Top with the third slice of toast and serve on lettuce.

Eggs and tomatoes

cooking time 20 minutes

you will need:

½ oz. butter	seasoning
1 teaspoon tomato ketchup	parsley
1 egg	

1 Melt the butter in an individual ovenproof dish.
2 Add the ketchup and a little chopped parsley.
3 Break the egg into the dish, season with salt and pepper, dot with a little more butter and bake in a moderate oven (350° F.—Gas Mark 4) until the egg is set.

Noodles tartare

cooking time about 12 minutes

you will need:

6 oz. noodles	2–3 tablespoons green
1 oz. butter	pepper, cut into strips,
2 teaspoons made mustard	or sliced mushrooms,
dash cayenne pepper	cooked in butter
dash white pepper	(optional)

1 Cook the noodles in plenty of fast boiling salted water for about 9 minutes until just soft but slightly firm to bite.
2 Drain and rinse under running cold water.
3 Return to the pan with the butter and seasoning and shake gently until piping hot. Add the green pepper or mushrooms if used.
4 Serve with cooked chicken, steak, lamb chops or veal.

Tomato pie

cooking time 25–30 minutes

you will need:

4 oz. potatoes
salt
1 oz. butter
1 tablespoon milk
3 oz. grated cheese

1 8-oz. can whole peeled tomatoes
2 tablespoons orange juice
pepper
2 level teaspoons chopped parsley

Peel the potatoes and boil in salted water until soft.

2 Drain and beat thoroughly with the butter and milk.
3 Add the grated cheese and beat until quite smooth and fluffy.
4 Pile the potato into a greased ovenproof dish, leaving a hollow in the centre of the potato.
5 Place under a hot grill until lightly browned— 2–3 minutes.
6 Strain the tomatoes and place with the orange juice, pepper and parsley in a saucepan. Heat through.
7 Serve in the centre of the potato.

Egg dishes

You need never be at a loss for ideas for a meal if you have eggs in the cupboard. Because of their nutritional value and the fact that they can be so easily and quickly prepared, eggs form the basis of many tempting dishes.
Apart from using eggs boiled, baked, poached or scrambled, once you have mastered the art of making an omelette you have the basis of a simple or sophisticated meal, depending on how you feel.

Poached eggs

Use a shallow pan containing enough water to cover the eggs by 1 inch.
Bring water to boil, reduce to simmering. Break egg into a cup, stir water then quickly slip egg into water.
Simmer for 3–5 minutes, depending on firmness wanted. Do not allow water to boil or the egg will be tough.
Remove egg with a perforated spoon. Allow it to drain, serve on a slice of hot buttered toast or on one of the following:
Cooked chopped spinach, coated with cheese sauce, browned under grill if liked
Rice, served with tomato or curry sauce
Risotto, served with tomato sauce if liked
Sweet corn niblets with tomato sauce if liked
Spaghetti
Toast covered with a thin cheese slice and grilled
Toast topped with mushrooms fried in butter
Toast topped with a slice of ham or cooked bacon
Toast topped with baked beans fried with a little chopped onion, or with curried beans
Potato cake fried with bacon
Fish cake

Baked eggs

1 Put $\frac{1}{2}$ oz. butter in the bottom of a small ovenproof dish. Place dish on a baking tray.
2 Place in a moderate oven until the butter has melted.
3 Break an egg into the dish, season lightly with salt and pepper.
4 Return to oven and bake until egg is set (5–8 minutes). Serve at once accompanied by toast or with cooked vegetables or salad. Alternatively sprinkle egg with 1 teaspoon finely grated cheese and cook under grill until yolk is just set, about 5 minutes.

Baked egg with potato

1 Grease a small ovenproof dish and line with 2–3 tablespoons creamed potato.
2 Break an egg into the centre, season lightly with salt and pepper. Sprinkle with grated cheese.
3 Bake in a moderate oven until set, about 20 minutes.

Baked Swiss egg

1 Grease a small ovenproof dish and line with thin slices cheese, preferably Gruyère.
2 Break egg over cheese. Season lightly.
3 Dot with butter, bake in a moderate oven 15–20 minutes.

To scramble eggs

1 Allow 2 eggs for 1 person.
2 Beat the eggs well. Add salt and pepper and a tablespoon of milk for each egg.
3 Melt just enough butter in a saucepan to cover the bottom of the pan. Before it is hot, put in the eggs and cook slowly over a very gentle heat. A double saucepan may be used if preferred or a basin in a saucepan with boiling water halfway up the sides of the basin.
4 As the eggs set on the bottom and sides of the pan, stir the flakes off gently with a spoon but avoid stirring more than is necessary to prevent eggs sticking to the pan.
5 Stir in additional ingredients if used.
6 Pile on hot buttered toast or straight on to a warm plate.

Note:
Scrambled eggs should be served as soon as they are set—about 5 minutes and they should be soft and creamy. Unless removed from the heat at once they tend to go on cooking.

Additional flavourings for scrambled eggs

For every 2 eggs add one of the following:
1 tablespoon diced sautéed bread cubes or cooked potato with ½ teaspoon chopped chives
1 cooked chicken liver, finely chopped and fried with chopped bacon
2 tablespoons chopped cooked ham, tongue or chicken
2 tablespoons flaked cooked fish
2 oz. chopped cooked mushrooms
1 tablespoon chopped parsley and chives
1½ oz. grated cheese
2–3 slices liver sausage, chopped
2 sliced cooked sausages or frankfurters

Omelettes

1 Allow 2 eggs for 1 person.
2 Beat the eggs lightly, just enough to mix the whites and yolks but no more.
3 Season with salt and pepper.
4 Heat just enough butter in the pan to cover the bottom—not more than ½ oz. for an 8-inch pan.
5 When the fat is very hot, pour in the eggs and cook briskly, stirring gently with a knife or fork. As the egg sets, slightly tilt the pan by raising the handle and push the set flakes towards the handle, thus allowing the liquid egg to run down on to the hot pan.

6 Immediately all is set, tilt the pan forward and roll the omelette over, turning in the edges.
7 Roll on to a very hot plate. Serve at once. If the omelette is to be filled, add the hot cooked filling such as chopped fried mushroom, tomato, bacon and so on, just before the omelette is rolled over. If a sweet omelette is required, fill with jam, previously warmed.
Do not make the omelette wait for its filling. From the moment the eggs starts to 'sizzle' in the pan until the omelette is ready for serving takes about 90 seconds. So make sure that the filling is ready when you start to cook the omelette. The centre of the omelette should be slightly 'runny' when the hot filling is added.

Omelette fillings

Cheese:
Grate 1½ oz. cheese. Mix 1 oz. with the eggs before cooking. Sprinkle the remainder over the cooked omelette, brown under a hot grill if liked.

Fish:
Use 2–3 tablespoons cooked fish. Chop fine, season with salt and blend with a little hot white sauce. Spread on the omelette before folding.

Ham, chicken or tongue:
Dice 2 oz. cooked meat, add to egg mixture before cooking.

Kidney:
Split 2 lambs' kidneys, remove skin and core. Sauté in 1 oz. butter. Dice cooked kidneys and add a little finely chopped cooked bacon or onion if liked. Pile mixture in centre of omelette before folding.

Onion:
Mix 1 tablespoon finely chopped onion and 1 teaspoon chopped parsley. Add to omelette mixture before cooking.

Fines herbes:
Add ½ teaspoon chopped fresh herbs, tarragon, chervil, parsley and chives, if liked, to the eggs before cooking.

Parsley:

Sprinkle finely chopped parsley over the centre of the omelette while cooking.

Mushroom:

Chop 2 oz. mushrooms. Sauté gently in 1 oz. butter until tender. Pile in centre of omelette before folding or add to egg mixture.

Potato:

Dice 1 cooked potato, add to egg mixture before cooking.

Tomato:

Skin and slice 2 tomatoes, season well. Cook in 1 dessertspoon oil or 1 oz. butter for 5 minutes. Add a good pinch mixed fresh herbs. Spoon over omelette before folding.

Sweet corn:

Heat 2-3 tablespoons sweet corn niblets or Mexicorn in the liquid from the can. Drain and spoon over omelette before folding. Or add 1 heaped tablespoon of corn to the eggs before cooking.

Left-overs:

Any of the following may be used as omelette fillings:

2-3 tablespoons cooked vegetables, heated up in a little white or cheese sauce.

2 tablespoons cooked macaroni or spaghetti heated in a little milk or butter.

2 tablespoons cooked rice or risotto, gently fried in butter or oil with a little finely chopped onion if liked.

3 heaped tablespoons condensed soup, heated with a tablespoon of milk or stock may be used as a filling or sauce. Mushroom, chicken or celery soups are especially good.

Sweet omelette:

Omit seasoning and add a good pinch castor sugar. Make as for savoury omelette; just before folding spread with 1 tablespoon jam or stewed or canned fruit. Dust with sugar and pop under a hot grill for a minute if liked.

Savoury eggs

cooking time about 30 minutes

you will need:

1 oz. butter or	2 eggs
1 dessertspoon olive oil	2 anchovy fillets
1 small can tomatoes	tomato sauce
tarragon vinegar	

1 Grease a shallow ovenproof dish with butter or oil.
2 Drain the tomatoes and place them in the bottom of the dish. Sprinkle very lightly with vinegar.
3 Break the eggs on to the tomatoes and bake until the eggs are set.
4 When cooked, top each egg with a warmed anchovy fillet and a little tomato sauce round the eggs.
5 Serve with triangles of toast.

Stuffed eggs Florentine

cooking time 10 minutes

you will need:

1 small packet frozen spinach	1 teaspoon chopped parsley or other flavouring
2 hard-boiled eggs	(see below)
1 oz. butter	$\frac{1}{4}$ pint cheese sauce
salt and pepper	(see page 69)
1 slice toast	

1 Cook spinach according to instructions on the packet. Drain well and put into the bottom of a small heatproof dish.
2 Cut each egg in half lengthways, remove yolk carefully with a teaspoon.
3 Mash the yolks with a fork, adding butter, salt and pepper to taste and parsley or other flavouring.
4 Put the yolk mixture back into the white, and place the two halves of each egg together again.
5 Place eggs on spinach, pour sauce over and brown under a hot grill or heat through in a moderate oven.
6 Serve with fingers of toast.
Any of the following may be added to the yolks in place of parsley:
$\frac{1}{2}$ oz. chopped lean ham, pinch mustard.
1 sardine, 2-3 drops vinegar.
1 tablespoon shrimps and chopped cress.
2 or 3 fillets of anchovy, chopped.
1 tablespoon chopped cooked mushrooms.

Stuffed egg salad

Prepare eggs as above, coat with mayonnaise instead of sauce, serve on lettuce, garnish with sliced tomato and cress.

Curried eggs (1)

cooking time about 1 hour

you will need:

1 onion, chopped	1 oz. cornflour
1 tablespoon corn oil	¾ pint boiling water
1 beef stock cube	1 dessertspoon red currant
1 apple, finely chopped	jelly
juice ½ lemon	1 tablespoons sultanas
2–3 eggs	2 level tablespoons
1 clove garlic, finely	desiccated coconut
chopped	infused in 6 tablespoons
2 level dessertspoons	boiling water
curry powder	chopped parsley
	4 oz. Patna rice

1 Hard-boil the eggs and leave in cold water.
2 Sauté the onion and garlic in the corn oil, stir in the curry powder and cornflour.
3 Cook for 3–4 minutes. Add the crumbled beef cube, water, apple, red-currant jelly, lemon juice and sultanas. Stir until boiling and simmer gently for 45 minutes.
4 Strain the liquor from the coconut and add to the sauce.
5 Shell and cut the eggs in half, pour the sauce over them, sprinkle with parsley and serve with the boiled rice.

This quantity makes 2 servings. For a simplified version of this dish, see following recipe.

Curried eggs (2)

cooking time 15 minutes if sauce is already prepared

you will need:

2 hard-boiled eggs	2 oz. rice
½ pint curry sauce (see	1 dessertspoon coconut
page 70)	(optional)

1 Cut eggs in half, add to sauce.
2 Simmer gently for 10–15 minutes.
3 Meanwhile boil rice in salted water until tender.
4 Drain rice and dry for a few minutes (see page 72).
5 Pile rice in a hot dish, top with eggs and sauce.
6 Sprinkle with coconut if liked or serve accompanied by coconut.

Diced cooked meat may be cooked in the same way.

Vegetables and Salads

Potato chips

Scrub and peel even-sized potatoes thinly. Cut into lengths about 2 inches long and ½ inch wide and thick. Place them in cold water as soon as they are cut. Rinse and drain them and dry in a clean cloth. Put into a frying basket and lower into the hot deep fat (360° F.). Cook until the potatoes are soft, but not brown, about 3 minutes. Lift out the basket and reheat the fat to 375° F. Place the basket back into the fat and fry until the potatoes are crisp and brown, about another 3 minutes. Drain on crumpled, absorbent paper, sprinkle with salt and serve at once.

Potato straws

Proceed as for potato chips, cutting the potatoes into straws about the size of a matchstick. Lower into hot fat and fry for 1 minute. Reheat the fat and fry the straws for about 2 minutes until crisp and brown. Drain on crumpled absorbent paper, sprinkle with salt and serve at once.

Sauté potatoes

Boil medium sized potatoes in their skins until they are just soft. Let them dry thoroughly, then peel and slice them ¼ inch thick. Heat 1–2 oz. butter or margarine in a frying pan, add the potatoes, sprinkle with salt and pepper and toss in the hot fat until lightly browned. Serve at once.

Mixed vegetables conservatively cooked

cooking time 30–45 minutes

you will need:

8 oz. mixed vegetables	⅛ pint boiling water
using those that are in	salt and pepper
season	chopped parsley
½ oz. butter or margarine	

1 Prepare the vegetables, cutting large ones into thin slices and halving the slices if necessary. If using young summer vegetables leave them whole if really small.
2 Melt the butter or margarine in a saucepan.

Add the vegetables and toss in the hot fat, starting with those that take the longest to cook. If using tomatoes do not add until 5 minutes before serving.

Add the boiling water using very little with summer vegetables.

Simmer gently until all the vegetables are tender.

Season and serve hot sprinkled with chopped parsley.

Baked onion

Peel 1 large onion and cook in boiling salted water for 20 minutes. Drain and place in an ovenproof dish. Sprinkle with salt and pepper and top with a knob of butter. Add enough milk to the dish to come $\frac{1}{3}$ way up the onion. Cover with greased paper and bake in a moderate oven (350° F.—Gas Mark 4) until tender, basting frequently with the milk. Serve with any liquor in the dish.

Baked mushrooms

Wash the mushrooms (as many as required) and peel the caps, trimming the stalks. Place in an ovenproof dish, gill sides uppermost. Sprinkle with salt, pepper and a little mace. Place a tiny piece of butter on each. Cover and cook in a moderately hot oven (375° F.—Gas Mark 5) for 25–30 minutes.

Baked tomatoes

Wash one large or two small tomatoes. Cut in half and place in a greased ovenproof dish. Season each with salt and pepper. Sprinkle each with a little sugar and a pinch of chopped tarragon—optional. Dot each half with a tiny piece of butter and cover with greased paper. Bake in a moderate oven (350° F.—Gas Mark 4), for about 20 minutes—until soft.

Leeks in white sauce

cooking time 15–20 minutes
you will need:

8 oz. leeks	$\frac{1}{4}$ pint white sauce (see
salt	page 68)

Remove the tops and roots of the leeks.

Cut the leeks into 1 inch lengths and wash thoroughly.

Place in a saucepan with about 1 inch cold water.

Bring to the boil, boil for 10–15 minutes until tender.

Drain well, sprinkle with salt and serve with white sauce poured over.

Braised onions

cooking time 45–50 minutes
you will need:

2 medium sized onions	$\frac{1}{4}$ pint white sauce
$\frac{1}{2}$ oz. melted butter	(see page 68)
seasoning	

1 Peel the onions, leaving them whole.
2 Place in a saucepan, cover with cold water, bring to the boil. Boil for 5 minutes and drain well.
3 Place in a well buttered ovenproof dish, and pour the melted butter over them. Season well with salt and pepper.
4 Bake in the centre of a moderate oven (350° F. —Gas Mark 4), basting occasionally during the cooking time.
5 Drain off the excess butter and serve with white sauce poured over the onions.

Carrots with parsley sauce

cooking time about 20 minutes
you will need:

6 oz. carrots	$\frac{1}{4}$ pint parsley sauce (see
salt	page 69)

1 If using new carrots, scrape them and leave them whole. Place in a pan of boiling salted water.
2 Boil until tender, drain well and serve with parsley sauce poured over.
If using old carrots, peel thinly and cut in half lengthways. Place in a pan, cover with cold water and $\frac{1}{2}$ level teaspoon salt. Bring to the boil and then cook as above.

Fried onion rings

cooking time 5 minutes
you will need:

1 large onion	1 tablespoon cold water
1 oz. flour	1 teaspoon lemon juice
bare $\frac{1}{4}$ teaspoon baking	1 tablespoon oil
powder	deep fat for frying
pinch salt	$\frac{1}{2}$ egg

1 Peel and slice the onion.
2 Sieve the flour, baking powder and salt into a bowl.
3 Beat the egg, lemon juice and water together.
4 Make a well in the centre of the flour, pour in the egg mixture and beat to a smooth batter.
5 Stir in the oil.
6 Dip the onion rings into the batter and fry in hot deep fat.
7 Drain well.

Braised celery

cooking time about 30 minutes

you will need:

1 small head of celery	little dripping
1 rasher bacon	seasoning
1 carrot	*bouquet garni*
1 small onion	stock

1 Prepare the celery and roughly cut up the bacon, carrot and onion.
2 Fry in the dripping until lightly browned. Add salt and pepper to taste, *bouquet garni* and enough stock to half cover.
3 Cover and cook gently until tender.
4 Drain and place the celery in a hot dish.
5 Boil the remaining liquid briskly until of a glazing consistency.
6 Pour over the celery and sprinkle with parsley.

Chicory with white sauce

cooking time 30–40 minutes

you will need:

1 large head chicory	salt
¼ pint white sauce (see page 68)	lemon juice

1 Cut off the hard end of the chicory and remove the outer leaves.
2 Split the head to within ½ inch of the end and wash well in cold water.
3 Place the chicory in a pan, just cover with water. Bring to the boil and boil for 5 minutes.
4 Drain and cook gently in boiling salted water until tender.
5 Add lemon juice to taste to the hot, well seasoned sauce.
6 Drain the chicory and place in a hot dish. Pour the sauce over and serve at once.

Boiled spinach

cooking time about 15 minutes

you will need:

1 lb. spinach	1 tablespoon cream
½ oz. butter	salt and pepper

1 Pick the spinach over carefully and wash in at least 3 changes of cold water. Break off the stalks, pulling out the centre stalks if they are tough.
2 Place the wet leaves in a saucepan, pressing well down. Do not add any water.
3 Cook gently until tender, stirring occasionally.
4 Drain well, pressing out all the water.
5 Reheat the spinach in the butter, adding the cream. Mix well and season to taste with salt and pepper.

Glazed carrots

cooking time about 30–45 minutes

you will need:

2–3 young carrots	pinch salt
knob butter	stock or water
lump sugar, if liked	chopped parsley

1 Scrape the carrots, leaving them whole.
2 Melt the butter, add the carrots, sugar, salt and enough boiling stock or water to come half way up the carrots.
3 Cook gently without a lid until tender, giving the pan an occasional shake.
4 When tender, remove the carrots and keep hot. Boil the remaining liquid until it is reduced to a glaze.
5 Add the carrots to the glaze, one at a time and turn them until they are well coated with the glaze.
6 Turn into a hot serving dish and sprinkle with chopped parsley.

Cauliflower mornay

cooking time about 25 minutes

you will need:

½ small cauliflower	¼ pint cheese sauce (see page 69)
salt	
½ oz. grated cheese	

1 Wash the cauliflower thoroughly, removing any tough outer leaves.
2 Make a deep slit in the stalk, using a sharp knife.
3 Place the cauliflower in boiling salted water and boil gently until tender.
4 Drain well and place in a hot dish. Pour the cheese sauce over the cauliflower, sprinkle with grated cheese and brown under a hot grill.

Cabbage in sour cream sauce

cooking time 12–15 minutes

you will need:

6 oz. white cabbage	1 teaspoon vinegar
½ small onion, finely chopped	seasoning
½ oz. butter	¼ pint sour cream sauce (see page 70)

1 Discard any tough leaves of cabbage and shred the remainder. Wash thoroughly.
2 Melt the butter, add the vinegar and about 1 teaspoon water. Bring to the boil.
3 Add the onion, cook for 2 minutes then add the cabbage. Cover and cook for about 10 minutes, shaking the pan frequently.
4 Season well with salt and pepper, pour on the sauce and serve.

Tuna coleslaw

you will need:

small white cabbage	1 tablespoon salad oil
heaped tablespoon shredded or chopped pineapple	salt and pepper
	1 large tomato
	3–4 anchovy fillets
tablespoon vinegar	2 heaped tablespoons tuna fish

Shred the cabbage as finely as possible.

Mix with the pineapple, vinegar, salad oil and a pinch of salt and pepper. This should be done 10 minutes before serving.

Arrange in a salad bowl, with tomato cut in slices.

Drain and flake the tuna, pile in centre of salad and place anchovy fillets on top of tuna.

Serve with thin slices brown bread and butter or with a baked potato.

Cooked flaked white fish may be used in place of tuna, and the salad dressed with mayonnaise instead of oil and vinegar.

Cheese and potato salad

you will need:

oz. new potatoes, cooked and sliced	lettuce
finely chopped spring onion or a few chives	2 tablespoons salad dressing
teaspoon chopped parsley	1½–2 oz. cheese, diced very small
	1 tomato

Slice the potatoes while still hot, add the finely chopped onion or chives, parsley and sufficient salad dressing to coat the potato. Chill.

Toss the cheese in the mixture very lightly.

Serve piled in the centre of a plate of crisp lettuce, and garnish with tomato quarters.

Beetroot salad

you will need:

small cooked beetroot	grated horseradish
French dressing (see page 70)	

Slice the beetroot and place in a bowl.

Sprinkle with freshly grated horseradish and pour on a little French dressing. Turn over once or twice and serve.

Green salad

Use two or more green salad plants such as lettuce, cress, watercress, endive, chicory, sorrel or cabbage.

Wash the salad quickly and thoroughly in fresh cold water and dry well.

Slice or shred those plants which require it and toss the salad in French dressing. To add extra flavour rub the serving bowl with a clove of garlic before putting in the salad and sprinkle with chopped parsley or other herbs.

Apple basket salad

you will need:

1 large red eating apple	1–2 oz. cheese
juice ½ lemon	2 tablespoons mayonnaise
2 sticks celery	watercress
1 tablespoon raisins or sultanas	

1 Scoop out flesh of apple with a sharp pointed knife.
2 Brush inside of apple with lemon juice to preserve colour.
3 Chop apple flesh, toss in remaining lemon juice.
4 Chop celery, dice cheese.
5 Mix apple, celery, cheese and dried fruit and toss lightly in mayonnaise.
6 Fill apple, garnish with watercress.
Chopped, cooked meat may be added to the apple filling if liked.

Cabbage and apple salad

you will need:

¼ small cabbage	juice ½ lemon
2 sticks celery	2 tablespoons mayonnaise
1 small eating apple	2–3 walnuts (optional)

1 Shred cabbage finely, chop celery.
2 Grate or finely chop apple, toss in lemon juice.
3 Toss salad ingredients together, adding mayonnaise.
4 Chop walnuts if used and sprinkle over salad.

Potato salad

you will need:

2–3 large new potatoes or waxy old potatoes	good pinch chopped parsley
2 tablespoons French dressing or mayonnaise	salt and pepper
	tomatoes or radishes
1 teaspoon chopped chives or spring onions	cress

1 Boil the potatoes in their jackets until they are just soft.
2 While they are hot, peel and cut into neat dice and mix with the dressing, spring onions or chives, parsley, salt and pepper to taste.
3 Pile on to a dish and garnish with overlapping slices of radish or tomato and cress.

Tomato salad

you will need:

2 tomatoes	1 teaspoon chopped chives
1 tablespoon French dressing (see page 70)	(optional)

1 Slice the tomatoes and place in a bowl.
2 On each later sprinkle some French dressing and a few chopped chives.

Chicken salad

you will need:

1 thick portion cooked chicken	1 teaspoon lemon juice
1 dessertspoon cream	paprika pepper
1 tablespoon mayonnaise	1 orange
	watercress

1 Remove the skin and bones from the chicken, keeping the portion as whole as possible.
2 Arrange in the centre of a flat dish.
3 Mix together the cream, mayonnaise and lemon juice and use to coat the chicken.
4 Sprinkle lightly with paprika pepper.
5 Remove the skin from the orange, cut into thin slices, removing any pips.
6 Arrange alternating slices of orange and sprigs of watercress round the chicken.
Cooked veal, lamb or ham may be used in place of chicken.

Minted salad

you will need:

4 oz. carrots	1 tablespoon mayonnaise
2 or 3 sticks celery if available	or salad cream
	$\frac{1}{2}$ teaspoon finely chopped
1 dessertspoon raisins	mint
lettuce	1 eating apple
lemon juice	

1 Scrape the carrots if necessary and grate them finely.
2 Wash and chop the celery.
3 Mix carrot, celery and raisins.
4 Arrange the lettuce on a plate, pile the carrot mixture in the centre.
5 Spoon the mayonnaise or salad cream over the carrot mixture, sprinkle with mint.
6 Garnish with apple, cut into slices and brushed with lemon juice.
Grated Cheddar cheese may be mixed with the carrot if liked.

Spanish salad

you will need:

3–4 lettuce leaves	2 oz. cooked ham or bacon
1 heaped tablespoon shredded white cabbage	3–4 stuffed olives
	4 anchovy fillets
1 tablespoon mayonnaise or salad cream	1 tomato

1 Arrange lettuce on a plate in a 'cup' shape.
2 Toss cabbage in mayonnaise, add ham, cut into strips, and olives chopped or sliced.
3 Pile in centre of lettuce, garnish with anchovy.
4 Arrange slices of tomato around the edge of the cabbage and serve.

Sunshine salad

you will need:

3–4 lettuce leaves	small bunch watercress
1 ring pineapple	1 or 2 cooked prunes
1 slice ham	1 heaped tablespoon cottage or cream chees

1 Arrange lettuce leaves on a plate and place th slice of ham in the centre.
2 Top with the pineapple ring and heap th cheese in the centre.
3 Garnish with watercress, and the prunes stoned and cut in half.

Orange basket salad

you will need:

1 large orange	1 tablespoon chopped
$\frac{1}{2}$ eating apple	celery
$\frac{1}{2}$ oz. walnuts, chopped	few sultanas or raisins
1 dessertspoon lemon juice	lettuce
2 tablespoons mayonnaise	

1 Cut the orange in half, scoop out the flesh with a teaspoon, removing pith and pips.
2 Chop the pulp from the orange if necessar and put it into a basin.
3 Chop the apple, toss in lemon juice, add t orange.
4 Add nuts, celery and dried fruit and tos lightly in mayonnaise.
5 Shred lettuce and use to line the orange skins
6 Pile the salad into the orange skins.
7 Serve as an accompaniment to cold meat o add cubes of cooked meat or cheese to th filling.

Nut and date salad

you will need:

1 ripe dessert pear	$\frac{1}{2}$ oz. chopped walnuts
juice $\frac{1}{2}$ lemon	parsley
1 small lettuce	French or salad dressing
1 oz. chopped dates	(see page 70)

1 Peel and halve the pear, remove the core and little of the flesh, to leave a hollow. Sprinkl the pear with lemon juice.
2 Wash the lettuce and shred a few of the leaves lining a salad plate with the remainder.
3 Place the shredded lettuce, dates, walnuts an chopped pear flesh and a little chopped parsle in a bowl. Toss in dressing.
4 Pile this mixture on the pear halves and plac on the lettuce.
If fresh pears are not available, well draine canned pears may be used.

Spring salad

you will need:

1 carrot, cooked	2–3 tablespoons French
1 tablespoon cooked peas	dressing (see page 70)
2 tablespoons cooked	lettuce
French beans	2 slices cold meat or 2 oz.
1 potato, cooked	grated cheese
salt and pepper	1 tomato

Dice the carrot and potato.

2 Cut the meat into strips or cube the cheese.

3 Mix the vegetables together, add a pinch of salt and pepper and sprinkle with French dressing. Leave in a cold place until required.

4 To serve, line an individual dish with lettuce leaves. Heap the vegetable mixture in the centre. Arrange the meat or cheese on top.

5 Garnish with tomato, cut into quarters or slices.

Russian salad

Prepare vegetables as in recipe for spring salad. Toss in mayonnaise. Serve on lettuce. Garnish with fillets of anchovy or slices of hard-boiled egg.

Celery and nut salad

you will need:

1 dessert apple	crisp-lettuce leaves—cos
juice ½ lemon	if possible
1 small celery heart	walnut halves
mayonnaise	raisins

1 Quarter the apple, remove the core and cut into thin slices. Toss in lemon juice.

2 Wash the celery and chop roughly.

3 Mix lightly with mayonnaise, adding a few walnuts and raisins.

4 Line a plate with crisp, well washed lettuce leaves and pile the salad in the centre.

Orange salad

you will need:

1 large orange	little chopped tarragon
good pinch castor sugar	and chervil, or chopped
1 dessertspoon French	mint
dressing (see page 70)	

1 Peel the orange and remove all the pith and pips. Cut into slices.

2 Place on a salad plate and sprinkle with castor sugar.

3 Pour the dressing over and sprinkle with tarragon and chervil if available, or with chopped mint.

4 Serve with cold meat or as an accompaniment to grilled fish.

Springtime fish salad

you will need:

4 oz. flaked cooked white	½ small lettuce
fish	mayonnaise or salad cream
salt and pepper	1 tablespoon cooked peas
lemon juice	1 tomato
1 teaspoon chopped mint	1 or 2 thin slices lemon
1 teaspoon chopped	
parsley	

1 Season fish to taste with salt, pepper and lemon juice.

2 Mix mint and parsley, add half to the fish with the peas.

3 Shred the outside lettuce leaves and place on a salad plate.

4 Pile the fish mixture on the lettuce, coat with mayonnaise.

5 Arrange the remainder of the lettuce, and the tomato cut into thin slices, round the fish.

6 Sprinkle with remaining mint and parsley and garnish with lemon slices, cut into quarters.

Herring salad

you will need:

1 small cooked potato	1 cooked herring
1 small cooked carrot	salad dressing
½ small cooked beetroot	lettuce
½ small apple	chopped parsley

1 Dice the potato, beetroot and apple.

2 Flake the herring, removing any bones.

3 Mix the diced vegetables, apple and herring.

4 Toss lightly in salad dressing.

5 Arrange lettuce on a plate, pile herring mixture in centre and sprinkle with chopped parsley.

Salmon salad

you will need:

2–3 tablespoons canned	mayonnaise or salad cream
salmon	1 hard-boiled egg
1 heaped tablespoon fresh	1 tomato
breadcrumbs	1 heaped tablespoon
vinegar	cooked peas
seasoning	lettuce or watercress

1 Drain salmon, mash with a fork and mix with breadcrumbs.

2 Add 2 or 3 drops of vinegar, salt and pepper to taste.

3 Shape into a mound on a salad plate, coat with mayonnaise or salad cream.

4 Arrange the hard-boiled egg and tomato, sliced, round the salmon. Sprinkle egg and tomato with salt and pepper.

5 Sprinkle the peas on top of the salmon.

6 Arrange small lettuce leaves or watercress in a ring round the salad and serve.

Prawn cocktail salad

you will need:

1 small lettuce heart
2 tablespoons picked prawns
1-inch piece cucumber
1 large tomato
mayonnaise
salt and pepper
cayenne pepper
slice lemon

1 Separate lettuce into small leaves, wash and dry well.
2 Arrange leaves in the bottom of a deep individual dish.
3 Place prawns, and cucumber peeled and sliced, on lettuce.
4 Skin tomato, remove seeds and chop finely or rub through a sieve, add salt and pepper to taste.
5 Blend tomato with sufficient mayonnaise to cover prawns.
6 Coat prawns with mayonnaise, dust with cayenne pepper.
7 Garnish with a thin slice of lemon, cut into 'butterflies'.
   To make lemon 'butterflies'. Cut slice of lemon in half. Cut each half almost through into quarters, cutting through the rind nearly to the centre. Open out to form 'wings'.

Puddings

Unless you have a sweet tooth, you probably will not take the time and trouble to cook a sweet course. There is no better way of finishing a meal than with fresh fruit, especially if you're watching your waist-line. If you don't have to count calories there are a selection of sweet recipes given here.

A single portion of ice cream or frozen mousse can be varied in many ways (see the chapter on entertaining). But these recipes needn't be saved for guests only; spoil yourself occasionally, you'll feel better for it.

Baked custard

cooking time 45 minutes

you will need:

1 egg
½ pint milk, warmed
1 tablespoon sugar
vanilla essence

1 Whisk eggs and sugar with a fork, adding a few drops of essence and milk, pour into a fireproof dish.
2 Bake in a slow oven (290° F. Gas Mark 1) for 45 minutes or until set.
   Enough for 2 servings.

Cup custard

cooking time about 15 minutes

you will need:

2 egg yolks
½ pint milk, short measure
1 dessertspoon sugar
few drops vanilla essence

1 Add a little cold milk to the egg yolks and heat the remainder of the milk.
2 Pour the hot milk over the lightly beaten yolks and milk, stirring well.
3 Return to the rinsed pan, and cook, stirring constantly, until the mixture coats the back of a spoon.
4 Add sugar and vanilla essence to taste.
5 Serve hot or cold. Enough for 2 servings.

Fruit trifle

you will need:

1 slice stale cake
2 teaspoons raspberry jam
½ small can fruit salad
¼ pint thick custard

1 Spread cake with jam and cut into cubes, place in a glass dish.
2 Drain juice from fruit and sprinkle over the cake. Arrange fruit, chopped if preferred, on the cake.
3 Pour cool custard over and leave until cold.

Thick custard

cooking time 10 minutes

you will need:

1½ level tablespoons custard powder
½ pint milk
1 rounded tablespoon sugar

1 Blend the custard powder with a little of the milk.
2 Bring the remaining milk to the boil.
3 Pour on to the blended custard, stirring all the time.
4 Rinse the pan with cold water, return the custard to the pan, and bring to the boil over a gentle heat, stirring all the time.
5 Boil for 2-3 minutes, add the sugar.
6 If cold custard is required, cover with a plate to prevent a skin forming.

Suggestions for using custard

Top a slice of Swiss roll with a heaped tablespoon of canned fruit. Allow juice to soak in for about 5 minutes. Pour over hot custard. Sprinkle with desiccated coconut if liked. Serve hot or cold.

Sandwich two thin slices Madeira cake with jam or stewed fruit. Pour hot custard over. Serve at once.

Whisk together ¼ pint thick cold custard with 2–3 tablespoons stewed fruit. Serve very cold accompanied by crisp biscuits.

Fill a canned peach half with raspberry jam or mincemeat. Place cut side down on a round of sponge cake. Pour custard over. Serve hot or cold.

Stir 1 sliced banana into ¼ pint custard. Sprinkle with grated chocolate. Serve cold.

Banana cream

cooking time 5 minutes

you will need:

2 level teaspoons custard powder	¼ pint milk
2 level teaspoons soft brown sugar	1 individual sponge cake
	2 tablespoons lemon juice
	1 banana

Blend the custard powder and sugar with 2 tablespoons of the milk.

Bring remaining milk to the boil, stir on to the blended custard powder, mix well and return to the pan. Cook gently, stirring all the time until thickened, about 2 minutes. Leave to cool.

Break the sponge into small pieces and place in the bottom of an individual glass dish.

Pour 1 tablespoon lemon juice over the cake and allow to stand for 5 minutes.

Peel the banana and slice thinly. Sprinkle with the remaining lemon juice.

Arrange the banana over the cake, reserving a few slices for decorating.

Pour the cooled custard over the banana and decorate with remaining slices.

Zabaglione

cooking time 10–15 minutes

you will need:

1 egg yolk	1 tablespoon castor sugar
1 tablespoon sweet sherry	2 Savoy finger biscuits

Put ingredients in a bowl over a pan of hot water except the biscuits.

2 Whisk until mixture becomes thick and creamy and holds the mark of the whisk.

3 Pile into a glass and serve immediately accompanied by Savoy finger biscuits.

Junket

cooking time 3–4 minutes

you will need:

⅓ pint milk	1 teaspoon rennet
1 teaspoon sugar	grated chocolate to decorate

1 Warm milk to blood heat, add the sugar and stir until dissolved.

2 Add the rennet and pour into a glass dish to set.

3 Decorate with grated chocolate or serve with stewed or fresh fruit.

Apple snowball

cooking time about 1 hour

you will need (per serving):

1 large apple	1 heaped teaspoon redcurrant jelly
1 egg white	
castor sugar	desiccated coconut

1 Peel and core the apple.

2 Brush with egg white and sprinkle with castor sugar.

3 Leave until dry, then repeat the process.

4 Place the apple in a pie dish, cover with a butter paper and bake in a slow oven (310° F. —Gas Mark 2) until tender, but not broken.

5 Remove carefully on to a serving plate, stuff the centre of the apple with jelly.

6 Sprinkle with coconut and serve.

Apple delight

cooking time about 10 minutes

you will need:

8 oz. cooking apples	3 tablespoons water
1 oz. sugar	½ packet orange jelly

1 Peel, core and slice the apples.

2 Add the water and sugar and stew over a gentle heat until the apples are tender.

3 Remove from heat, whisk with a fork and add the jelly broken into cubes.

4 Continue to whisk until the jelly is dissolved.

5 Pour into a mould and leave in a cold place until set.

6 Turn out and serve accompanied by a crisp biscuit. This amount is sufficient for 2 servings.

Jellied mandarins

cooking time 5 minutes

you will need:

5 tablespoons lemon squash
¼ pint water
4 level teaspoons gelatine
3 rounded teaspoons sugar
1 heaped tablespoon mandarin oranges

1 Put the water, gelatine and sugar in a small pan, stir over a gentle heat until the gelatine is dissolved. Take care that the mixture does not come to the boil.
2 Remove from heat, stir in the lemon squash and leave in cool place until beginning to set.
3 Stir in the oranges, pour into a rinsed ½-pint mould.
4 Leave in a cool place until set. Turn out and serve with cream if liked. This amount is enough for 2 servings.

Fruit and custard tart

cooking time about 30 minutes

you will need:

4 oz. shortcrust pastry (see page 67)
¼ pint milk
1 rounded dessertspoon custard powder
1 level dessertspoon sugar
2 tablespoons stewed fruit
1 teaspoon chopped almonds (optional)

1 Roll out pastry and use to line a deep pie plate, about 5 inches in diameter.
2 Bake 'blind' in a hot oven (400° F.—Gas Mark 6) for 15 minutes, remove foil and filling and put back in the oven for 5 minutes.
3 Meanwhile blend the custard powder with a little of the milk.
4 Bring the remainder of the milk to the boil, pour on to the blended custard powder, stirring all the time.
5 Return to the saucepan, rinsed out with cold water, cook for 3 minutes stirring continuously, add sugar.
6 If the tart is to be eaten at once, spread the bottom with fruit, pour the custard over, taking care that the hot custard does not run over on to the edge of the pastry.
7 Sprinkle with almonds if used and serve immediately.
8 To serve the tart cold, the pastry should be cold before adding the fruit, and the custard should be very cool before pouring into the pastry. Leave until really cold before serving.

Baked semolina custard

cooking time 40 minutes

you will need:

¼ pint milk
3½ teaspoons semolina
2 rounded teaspoons sugar
nutmeg
1 teaspoon custard powder
1 dessertspoon currants (optional)

1 Blend the custard powder with a little milk.
2 Boil the remainder of the milk, sprinkle in the semolina and cook over a gentle heat for 5 minutes, stirring.
3 Stir in the blended custard powder and cook for a further 5 minutes, stirring throughout.
4 Add sugar and vanilla essence to taste.
5 Sprinkle the currants if used over the bottom of a small greased pie dish, pour in the semolina mixture.
6 Grate nutmeg over the top, bake in a moderate oven (350° F.—Gas Mark 4) for 30 minutes. Serve hot or cold.

Honey custard

Spread honey thinly over the bottom of a pie dish, prepare mixture as above, pour over honey, sprinkle with cinnamon instead of nutmeg. Serve with thin slices of orange.

Almond dessert mould

cooking time 10 minutes

you will need:

¼ pint milk
1 dessertspoon semolina
1¼ teaspoons gelatine
3 teaspoons water
1 dessertspoon sugar
almond essence
raspberry or cherry jam

1 Bring the milk to the boil, sprinkle in the semolina, simmer for 10 minutes, stirring throughout.
2 Dissolve the gelatine in the water over a low heat.
3 Remove semolina from heat, stir in sugar and gelatine.
4 Add the essence a drop at a time, tasting to ensure that flavour is right.
5 Rinse a small mould (a teacup can be used) with cold water. Put a good teaspoonful of jam into the mould.
6 Pour in the semolina mixture and leave until cold.
7 Turn out and serve with thin cream if liked.

Syrup tart

cooking time 25 minutes

you will need:

oz. shortcrust pastry
 (see page 67)
dessertspoons syrup

1–2 oz. breadcrumbs
1 teaspoon lemon juice

Line a small ovenproof plate with pastry.
Blend the other three ingredients together and spread over pastry.
Re-roll remaining pastry and cut into thin strips, arrange in a lattice over the tart.
Bake in a hot oven (400° F.—Gas Mark 6) until golden. Serve hot or cold. This amount is sufficient for 2 servings.
Jam or stewed fruit may be used instead of syrup and cake crumbs may replace breadcrumbs.

Chocolate orange jelly

cooking time 10 minutes

you will need:

packet orange jelly
tablespoons water
pint milk, less
 2 tablespoons

1 teaspoon grated
 chocolate

Melt the jelly in the water over a very low heat.
Remove from heat and allow to become cold but not set.
Slowly stir in the milk.
Pour into a mould rinsed with cold water, leave in a cold place until set.
Turn out and sprinkle with grated chocolate.
This amount is enough for 2 servings.

Fruit tartlets

cooking time about 25 minutes

you will need:

2 oz. shortcrust pastry
 (see page 67)
2 oz. fresh fruit, as
 available
3 level teaspoons sugar

2 rounded teaspoons jam
milk
extra sugar

Stone the fruit if necessary, chop and cook in a little water, with sugar added, until fruit is tender.
Drain fruit and leave until cold.
Roll out pastry and use to line two patty or bun tins.
Spread jam in the bottom of each and top with fruit.
Re-roll remaining pastry, cut into strips and arrange in a lattice over each tartlet.
Brush with milk, sprinkle with extra sugar.

7 Bake in a hot oven (400° F.—Gas Mark 6) until golden.
8 Serve hot or cold.
Drained canned fruit may be used instead of fresh fruit, mincemeat or marmalade instead of jam.

Apple delight

you will need:

5-oz. carton yoghurt
1 eating apple
1 dessertspoon lemon juice
little lemon rind

castor sugar to taste
few chopped walnuts
few black and green
 grapes (optional)

1 Empty yoghourt into a basin, add grated lemon rind and juice, sugar and walnuts.
2 Grate apple into mixture, stir lightly.
3 Pile in individual glass dish and serve chilled if possible.

Muesli

you will need:

1 tablespoon rolled oats
1 tablespoon ground nuts
1 dessertspoon raisins

1 apple
honey (optional)

1 Soak oats in water overnight, or in milk for 30 minutes before required, according to taste.
2 Add nuts and raisins.
3 Grate apple and stir quickly into mixture.
4 Serve at once, adding a little honey if liked.
If muesli is prepared with water it may be served with cream or evaporated milk. Cooked dried apricots or sliced banana may be added with apple.
This is also an excellent breakfast dish.

Gooseberry fool

cooking time 20 minutes

you will need:

8 oz. gooseberries
1 tablespoon water
2 oz. sugar

$\frac{1}{4}$ pint double cream or
 thick custard

1 Top and tail the gooseberries and cook in the water.
2 When nearly tender, add the sugar.
3 When soft, pass through a sieve and allow to become cold.
4 Whip the cream slightly and fold into the gooseberry purée.
5 Pour into an individual dish and serve very cold. Enough for 2 servings.

Summer pudding

cooking time 5–10 minutes

you will need:

2 oz. sliced, stale bread or plain cake

2 oz. sugar

custard (see page 42) or fruit juice, to coat

8 oz. any soft fruit or mixture of soft fruit

arrowroot (for thickening)

1 Cut the bread or cake into thin fingers 1 inch wide and use to line the sides of a ½-pint pudding basin.

2 Cut triangles for lining the bottom.

3 Cook the chosen fruit with as little water as possible until it has become a pulp. Sweeten to taste.

4 Pour the fruit into the lined basin or dish. Cover the top with slices of bread or cake.

5 Cover with a saucer topped with a weight and leave for several hours, overnight if possible, in a cold place.

6 Turn out and coat with custard or fruit juice thickened to a coating consistency with arrowroot (1 level teaspoon to ¼ pint juice).

7 Serve at once.

Apple crumble

cooking time 20–30 minutes

you will need:

8 oz. apples

1 oz. brown sugar

grated lemon rind (optional)

1 oz. butter or margarine

2 oz. plain flour

1 oz. castor sugar

1 Peel, core and slice the apples into a pan. Add about 2 tablespoons water, the brown sugar and a little grated lemon rind if liked.

2 Cover and cook gently until the apples are soft.

3 When cooked, turn into a greased pie dish.

4 Rub the butter or margarine into the flour, add the sugar and mix well.

5 Sprinkle this mixture over the apple and press down lightly.

6 Cook in a moderate oven (350° F. Gas Mark 4), until golden brown.

7 When cooked, sprinkle with castor sugar if liked, and serve with cream or custard.

Alternatives

Rhubarb, pears, plums or gooseberries may be used in place of apples. A crumble topping may also be added to canned fruit; cook for 15–20 minutes until topping is cooked, omit brown sugar and extra castor sugar. Add syrup from the fruit in place of water.

Apricot rice pudding

cooking time 1½ hours

you will need:

½ oz. rice

⅓ pint milk

½ oz. sugar

2 oz. castor sugar

knob butter

1 teaspoon apricot jam

1 egg white

1 Place the rice in the top of a double saucepan with the milk, sugar and butter and allow to cook for about 1 hour, or until the rice is thick and creamy.

2 Turn the rice on to a pie dish.

3 Warm the jam and spread it over the rice.

4 Whisk the egg white until stiff, then whisk in half the sugar.

5 Fold in the remaining half and spread the meringue over the rice.

6 Sprinkle with a little castor sugar and bake in a moderate oven (350° F. — Gas Mark 4), for about 30 minutes.

Clementine pudding

cooking time about 35 minutes

you will need:

⅓ pint milk

½ oz. semolina

about ½ teaspoon grated lemon rind

1 oz. castor sugar

1 egg

2-3 slices orange

1 Bring the milk to the boil, sprinkle in semolina and finely grated lemon rind to taste.

2 Allow to boil for about 15 minutes, stirring frequently.

3 Remove from heat, stir in three-quarters of the sugar and the egg yolk.

4 Whisk egg white until stiff, fold into mixture.

5 Pour into greased dish and bake in a moderate oven (350° F. — Gas Mark 4), until golden.

6 Decorate with thin slices of orange sprinkled with remaining sugar.

Topsy pudding

Use orange rind in place of lemon rind. Sprinkle cooked pudding with coarsely grated plain chocolate.

Sugar 'n' spice pudding

Use ½ oz. castor sugar when making pudding. Sprinkle pudding with brown sugar mixed with a pinch of mixed spice during last 5 minutes of cooking.

Baked apple

cooking time 45 minutes – 1 hour

you will need:

1 large cooking apple	*filling:*
½ oz. demerara sugar	½ oz. moist brown sugar,
water	creamed with ½ oz.
	butter

1 Wash the apple and remove the core.
2 Cut round the skin of the apple with the tip of a knife about two-thirds up from the base.
3 Stand the apple in an ovenproof dish and fill with the creamed butter and sugar.
4 Sprinkle the apple with demerara sugar and add 2 tablespoons of water to the dish.
5 Bake in a moderate oven (350° F.—Gas Mark 4) until the apple is soft in the centre.
6 Serve with custard or cream if liked.

Alternative fillings:

Apricot jam mixed with a few chopped, blanched almonds
Mincemeat
Chopped, stoned dates, mixed with honey and a pinch of cinnamon
Sultanas, currants or raisins mixed with sugar

Apple meringue

cooking time 30 minutes

you will need:

2 oz. fresh white	¼ pint milk
breadcrumbs	4 oz. castor sugar
1 egg, separated	1 large cooking apple

1 Place the breadcrumbs in a 1-pint oven glass basin, previously greased.
2 Beat the egg yolk and milk together. Add 2 oz. of the sugar.
3 Pour this mixture over the breadcrumbs and allow to stand for 10 minutes.
4 Peel, core and grate the apple and arrange over the top of the soaked breadcrumbs.
5 Whisk the egg white until stiff, add the sugar and re-whisk until stiff again.
6 Pile on top of the apple and bake in the lower half of a moderately hot oven (375° F.—Gas Mark 5), until the meringue is crisp.
Canned fruit may be used in place of apple, add only 1 oz. sugar to breadcrumbs.

Baked coconut pudding

cooking time 35 minutes

you will need:

1 oz. fresh breadcrumbs	2½ oz. castor sugar
½ oz. butter	1 egg
¼ pint milk	1 dessertspoon desiccated
little grated lemon rind	coconut
1 teaspoon jam	

1 Place the breadcrumbs, ½ oz. sugar, coconut, and lemon rind in a bowl.
2 Heat the milk and butter and pour over the dry ingredients. Leave to stand for 5 minutes.
3 Add the beaten egg yolk and pour into a greased pie dish.
4 Bake in a moderate oven (350° F.—Gas Mark 4), for about 20 minutes until set.
5 Whisk the white stiffly, fold in half the remaining sugar, and whisk again. Fold in the rest of the sugar.
6 Spread jam on top of the pudding, cover with meringue, and return to a slow oven (310° F.—Gas Mark 2), until beginning to brown.

Pineapple upside-down pudding

cooking time 40 minutes

you will need:

6 oz. butter	4 oz. castor sugar
2 oz. soft brown sugar	2 eggs, beaten
2 canned pineapple rings	4 oz. plain flour
2 tablespoons juice (from	1 level teaspoon baking
the pineapple)	powder
1 glacé cherry	

1 Melt 2 oz. butter, stir in the brown sugar and mix well.
2 Spread on the bottom of a 5-inch cake tin.
3 Halve the pineapple rings and arrange over the mixture. Cut the cherry into four and decorate the base of the tin.
4 Cream the remaining butter in a bowl, add the castor sugar and beat until light and fluffy.
5 Gradually add the beaten egg to the creamed mixture.
6 Sieve the flour and baking powder together and fold lightly into the creamed mixture using a metal spoon.
7 Add the pineapple juice, mix well and spread the mixture over the pineapple.
8 Bake in the centre of a hot oven (400° F.—Gas Mark 6) until golden brown and firm to the touch. Reduce to 350° F.—Gas Mark 4—after 15 minutes.
9 Allow to cool slightly then turn out on to a hot dish. Serve with cream. Makes enough for 2 servings.
If preferred, the pudding may be baked in two individual dishes, placing a whole pineapple ring in the bottom of each with a half glacé cherry in the centre of each ring.

Mandarin meringue pudding

cooking time 20–30 minutes

you will need:

1 individual sponge cake	2½ oz. castor sugar
½ can mandarin oranges	¼ pint milk
1 egg	

1 Cut the sponge cake in half lengthways and place in bottom of an ovenproof dish.
2 Cover with mandarins, adding enough juice to moisten the cake.
3 Separate the yolk from the white of the egg.
4 Beat the yolk with ½ oz. of the sugar. Heat the milk and pour on to the yolk, stirring.
5 Return to the pan (rinsed out in cold water) and cook over a gentle heat until the custard thickens. Pour over the cake and fruit.
6 Whisk the egg whites until stiff. Fold in 1 oz. sugar and whisk again until stiff. Fold in remaining sugar.
7 Pile on top of the pudding and bake in a cool oven (310° F.—Gas Mark 2), until the meringue is crisp.

Bread pudding

cooking time about 30 minutes

you will need:

2 oz. stale bread	½ oz. sugar
1 oz. raisins or sultanas	½ large egg
½ oz. shredded suet	milk
nutmeg	

1 Remove crusts and cut bread into small pieces. Soak in warm water for 30 minutes.
2 Drain, squeeze out moisture with a wooden spoon. Beat out lumps with a fork.
3 Add sultanas, suet and sugar. Mix with beaten egg and a little milk if necessary to make a soft mixture.
4 Spoon into a greased pie dish and sprinkle with grated nutmeg.
5 Bake in a moderate oven (350° F.—Gas Mark 4), until golden brown.
6 Sprinkle with castor sugar and serve hot.

Fresh fruit salad

cooking time about 5 minutes

you will need:

to each 8 oz. fruit allow	1½–2 oz. sugar
½ pint water or fruit	juice ½ lemon
juice	fresh fruit as available

1 Prepare the syrup by boiling the water or fruit juice, lemon juice and the sugar together until it is reduced to half the quantity.
2 Prepare the fruit according to its kind. Apples should be peeled, cored and sliced. If liked, the skin of a red-skinned apple can be left on for colour. Oranges should be skinned and all traces of pith removed. The quarters can be halved if liked. Remove the skins and seeds from grapes, leaving a few black grapes unpeeled for colour.
3 Place the prepared fruit in a bowl and pour syrup over. Cover the bowl and leave to become cold.
4 Sliced bananas may be added just before serving.

Chocolate mousse

cooking time 10 minutes

you will need:

2 oz. plain chocolate	1 tablespoon whipped
1 egg	cream (optional)
1 teaspoon brandy (optional)	

1 Break the chocolate into a basin over a pan of hot water.
2 Separate the egg. Add the yolks and brandy, if used, to the chocolate when melted.
3 Stir well and allow to heat gently until the mixture is fairly thick.
4 Remove from heat and allow to cool but not to set.
5 Whisk egg white until stiff, fold into chocolate. Pour into a glass. Decorate with cream if liked.

Fruit pudding

cooking time 2½ hours

you will need:

2 oz. plain flour	2 oz. soft brown sugar
pinch salt	pinch mixed spice
1 level teaspoon baking powder	2 oz. currants
	2 oz. raisins
2 oz. fresh white breadcrumbs	1 egg, beaten
	2 tablespoons milk
2 oz. shredded suet	

1 Grease a 1-pint pudding basin.
2 Sieve the flour, salt and baking powder into a bowl.
3 Add the breadcrumbs, suet, sugar, mixed spice, currants and raisins.
4 Beat the egg and milk together and stir into the flour mixture.
5 When the mixture is quite smooth, turn into the prepared basin, cover with greased greaseproof paper and boil gently until cooked.
Enough for 2 servings. To reheat, steam or fry in butter, serve sprinkled with brown sugar or with thin custard.

Cakes and biscuits

Victoria sandwich

cooking time 25 minutes

you will need:

4 oz. butter or margarine	4 oz. self-raising flour
4 oz. sugar	water or milk, about
2 eggs	1 tablespoon (optional)

1 Grease two 7-inch sandwich tins and dust with flour.
2 Cream the fat and sugar.
3 Beat in the eggs gradually.
4 Fold in the sieved flour.
5 Divide between the two tins making sure the mixture is level.
6 Bake on the top shelf of a moderately hot oven (375° F.—Gas Mark 5).
7 Turn out on to a wire rack to cool. When cold, sandwich together with jam and dust the top with sugar.

Note:

If large eggs are used, additional liquid is not necessary, but water or milk may be added with the egg to give a soft dropping consistency. For 8-inch sandwich tins you will need: 3 eggs and 6 oz. fat, sugar and self-raising flour. Bake for 30–35 minutes.

Rich fruit cake

(also suitable for a Christmas cake)

cooking time about 1½ hours

you will need:

4 oz. raisins	1 oz. cornflour
4 oz. sultanas	¼ teaspoon salt
2 oz. currants	1 level teaspoon
2 oz. glacé cherries	bicarbonate of soda
1 oz. chopped mixed peel	2 tablespoons sherry
1 oz. blanched chopped	1 level teaspoon cocoa
almonds	1 level teaspoon mixed
4 oz. dark, soft brown sugar	spice
4 oz. butter	½ teaspoon each vanilla,
2 eggs	almond and lemon
6 oz. plain flour	essence

1 Set oven at 335° F.—Gas Mark 3. Line a 5½-inch square, or 6-inch round, cake tin with greaseproof paper.
2 Prepare and mix the fruits and almonds.

3 Cream the butter and sugar.
4 Sieve the dry ingredients, including cocoa and spice.
5 Dissolve the soda in the sherry.
6 Add 2 teaspoons of the dry ingredients to the creamed mixture then add the eggs one at a time, beating well between each.
7 Add the dry ingredients, the soda and sherry, the fruit and flavourings.
8 Spoon mixture into cake tin and spread evenly.
9 Bake on the bottom shelf of the oven at 335° F.—Gas Mark 3, reducing to 310° F.—Gas Mark 2 after the first 30 minutes.

Everyday fruit cake

This cake improves with keeping and is an excellent standby for the cake tin

cooking time about 2 hours

you will need:

1 lb. flour	3 oz. glacé cherries,
1 level teaspoon salt	quartered
8 oz. castor sugar	4 oz. chopped mixed peel
6 oz. margarine	2 level teaspoons
8 oz. currants	bicarbonate of soda
6 oz. sultanas	½ pint milk
4 oz. seedless raisins	3 tablespoons malt vinegar

1 Grease a 7-inch round tin, place a round of greased greaseproof paper in the bottom.
2 Sieve flour and salt into a bowl and add the sugar.
3 Rub in fat until mixture resembles breadcrumbs.
4 Stir in fruit.
5 Dissolve the bicarbonate of soda in milk and add the vinegar.
6 Stir quickly into the dry ingredients using a wooden spoon. Beat until well mixed and smooth.
7 Turn into tin and smooth top with a palette knife.
8 Bake in the centre of a moderate oven (350° F.—Gas Mark 4). Cover cake with a double sheet of greaseproof paper after the first hour, to prevent over-browning.
9 Turn out on to a wire try to cool.

One-stage cake

cooking time 25–35 minutes

you will need:

4 oz. self-raising flour	4 oz. sugar
1 level teaspoon baking powder	2 eggs
4 oz. luxury margarine, softened	filling and icing as liked

1 Grease two 7-inch sandwich tins and line the bottom of each with a round of greaseproof paper.
2 Sieve flour and baking powder into a bowl.
3 Put the margarine and sugar into the bowl.
4 Break the eggs into the bowl. Mix all the ingredients together with a wooden spoon— this should take about 1 minute.
5 Divide the mixture between the tins. Bake at 335° F. Gas Mark 3—on the middle shelf.
6 When the cakes are cold, sandwich together with creamy filling and coat the top with icing (see page 56).
If liked, the cake may be baked in one 8-inch cake tin, greased and the bottom lined with greaseproof paper. Cook for 35–45 minutes.

Uncooked chocolate cake

you will need:

4 oz. luxury margarine	*glacé icing:*
1 oz. castor sugar	6 oz. sieved icing sugar
1 tablespoon golden syrup	2–3 dessertspoons hot water
3 level tablespoons cocoa	
8 oz. crushed sweet biscuits	1–2 drops red colouring
	1 yard ribbon

1 Melt the margarine, sugar and syrup in a pan, but do not boil.
2 Put the cocoa and crushed biscuits into a mixing bowl and add the melted ingredients. Mix all together.
3 Turn the mixture into a greased 8-inch sandwich tin and press down well. Smooth the top with a palette knife.
4 Leave to set (preferably in a refrigerator) overnight.
5 Put the sieved icing sugar into a bowl and mix to a coating consistency with the hot water. Place 1 tablespoon of the icing in a small bowl and add red colouring.
6 Turn the cake out of the tin and coat the top with the white icing.
7 While the icing is still wet, pipe lines of pink icing across the cake about $\frac{1}{4}$ inch apart.
8 With a pointed knife or skewer, draw lines at

right angles across the pink icing to give a feathered effect.
9 When set, tie a ribbon round the sides of the cake.

Spicy pastry cakes

cooking time 15–20 minutes

you will need:

6 oz. shortcrust pastry (see page 6)	4 oz. currants
	1–2 oz. chopped peel
egg white to glaze	good pinch grated nutmeg
castor sugar	good pinch mixed spice
filling:	1 oz. sugar
1 oz. butter	

1 Make the filling by melting the butter and adding the fruit, sugar and spice.
2 Roll out the pastry $\frac{1}{8}$ inch thick and cut into rounds with a large cutter.
3 Place a spoonful of filling on each round. Damp the edges of the pastry and draw them together to enclose the filling.
4 Turn cakes over so that the smooth side is uppermost, flatten slightly with the rolling pin. Make 3 cuts across the top of each.
5 Place on a baking tray, brush with egg white and dredge with castor sugar.
6 Bake at 400° F.—Gas Mark 6—until golden. Cool on a wire tray.

Almond flapjacks

cooking time 20 minutes

you will need:

2 level tablespoons sugar	4 oz. quick porridge oats
2 oz. margarine	1 tablespoon ground almonds
1 tablespoon golden syrup	
$\frac{1}{4}$ teaspoon almond essence	

1 Grease a 6-inch sandwich tin.
2 Heat sugar, margarine and syrup in a pan over a gentle heat.
3 When fat has melted and the sugar dissolved, stir in the oats, almonds and essence.
4 Turn mixture into prepared tin and press down evenly.
5 Bake at 375° F.—Gas Mark 5—until firm and golden.
6 Cut into 8 pieces while warm.
7 Leave to cool and remove pieces separately on to a wire tray. Leave until cold.

Bakewell tart

cooking time 30–40 minutes

you will need:

4 oz. shortcrust pastry (see page 67)	1 egg
	2 oz. ground almonds
raspberry jam	1–2 drops almond essence
2 oz. butter	icing sugar
2 oz. sugar	

1 Line a flan tin or sandwich tin with shortcrust pastry, spread with jam.
2 Cream butter and sugar, gradually beat in the egg.
3 Add the essence.
4 Stir in the almonds and spread the mixture over the jam.
5 Bake in a hot oven (400° F.—Gas Mark 6), until the filling is set and golden.
6 Dredge with icing sugar.

Swiss tarts

cooking time 30 minutes

you will need:

4 oz. butter or margarine	4 oz. flour
1 oz. castor sugar	icing sugar
2–3 drops vanilla essence	apricot jam or glacé cherries

1 Sieve the flour.
2 Cream the fat and sugar until light and fluffy, adding the vanilla essence.
3 Fold in the sieved flour.
4 Using a forcing bag and a large star nozzle, pipe the mixture into paper cases on a baking sheet. Start at the centre of the bottom of each case and pipe with a spiral movement round the sides, leaving a shallow depression in the centre.
5 Bake at 375° F.—Gas Mark 5. Cool on a wire tray.
6 When tarts are cold, dust with icing sugar and fill centre with a teaspoon apricot jam or a halved glacé cherry.

Honeybee biscuits

cooking time 10–15 minutes

you will need:

4 oz. butter	4 oz. plain flour
2 level tablespoons honey	chopped glacé cherries or
$\frac{1}{4}$ teaspoon vanilla essence	chopped toasted almonds

1 Cream butter and honey until light and fluffy, add vanilla essence and mix well. Add sieved flour gradually.
2 Flour hands and roll small amounts of mixture into balls of three sizes.
3 Place three balls together one under the other on a greased baking sheet to form one biscuit.
4 Flatten slightly and sprinkle with chopped cherries or almonds.
5 Bake in a moderately hot oven (375° F.—Gas Mark 5). Cool on a wire tray.

Truffle cakes

you will need:

4 oz. stale sponge cake	almond or rum essence
4 oz. castor sugar	(optional)
4 oz. ground almonds	chocolate icing (see page
apricot jam	64) or melted chocolate
chocolate vermicelli	

1 Grate the cake into crumbs or rub through a coarse sieve into a mixing bowl.
2 Add the sugar and almonds.
3 Warm the jam over a gentle heat and sieve.
4 Blend the cake and almond mixture to a firm paste with the jam, adding a few drops almond or rum essence if liked.
5 Shape the mixture into 12–18 balls and leave in a cool place until firm.
6 Dip each ball in glacé icing or melted chocolate using a skewer.
7 Roll in chocolate vermicelli and leave on a plate until dry.
8 Serve in small paper cases.

Coconut pyramids

cooking time 45 minutes

you will need:

2 egg whites	5 oz. desiccated coconut
5 oz. sugar	glacé cherries

1 Grease a baking sheet. Cut small rounds of rice paper, if liked, about 2 inches in diameter and place on the baking sheet.
2 Whisk egg whites stiffly and fold in sugar and coconut. Tint half the mixture pink if liked.
3 Pile mixture on rounds of paper or on to the baking sheet. Form into pyramid shapes.
4 Bake in a slow oven (265° F.—Gas Mark $\frac{1}{2}$), until touched with gold. Top each with a glacé cherry, halved, half way through the cooking time.
5 Cool on a wire tray. Trim rice paper if necessary.

Chocolate coconut pyramids

Make as above, omitting cherries. Allow the pyramids to cool and then top each with a teaspoon melted chocolate. Allow chocolate to run down the sides a little and set.

51

Sherry frosted cakes

cooking time 15 minutes

you will need:

2 oz. plain flour	2 eggs
2 oz. fine semolina	¼ teaspoon vanilla essence
2 oz. ground almonds	¼ teaspoon almond essence
1 teaspoon baking powder	1 oz. chopped walnuts
pinch salt	sherry icing
4 oz. butter	glacé cherries or walnuts
2 oz. castor sugar	(optional)

1 Grease 20 small patty tins.
2 Sieve the first five ingredients.
3 Melt butter and allow to cool slightly.
4 Stir in sugar, well beaten eggs and essence.
5 Stir in dry ingredients and chopped walnuts.
6 Two-thirds fill prepared tins.
7 Bake at 375° F.—Gas Mark 5, until golden.
8 When cold, place a spoonful of sherry icing on top of each, swirling it with the back of the spoon if liked.
9 Decorate with half a glacé cherry or walnut if liked.

Sherry icing

Blend 4 heaped tablespoons icing sugar with 1½ tablespoons sherry.

Fruit and nut delights

Make cakes as above. Just before serving spread top with double cream whisked until thick and decorate with drained canned fruit. Sliced peaches or mandarin oranges are particularly good.

Date and nut bread

cooking time 1¾ hours

you will need:

8 oz. flour	3 oz. chopped dates
3 level teaspoons baking powder	2 oz. black treacle
	1½ oz. chopped walnuts
¾ level teaspoon salt	1 oz. butter
½ level teaspoon bicarbonate of soda	¼ pint milk
2 oz. soft brown sugar	

1 Grease and line a 2-lb. loaf tin.
2 Sieve the flour, salt, baking powder and bicarbonate of soda into a bowl. Add the dates and nuts.
3 Heat the sugar, treacle, butter and milk gently until the sugar dissolves, stirring carefully.
4 Stir with a metal spoon into the dry ingredients, mixing well. Do not beat.
5 Pour the batter into the prepared tin.
6 Bake in a moderate oven (350° F.—Gas Mark 4). This bread will keep moist. Serve sliced with butter.

Welsh cakes

cooking time about 12 minutes

you will need:

4 oz. flour	1 oz. lard
¼ teaspoon baking powder	1 oz. currants
2 oz. margarine	milk to mix

1 Sieve the flour and baking powder.
2 Rub in the margarine and lard, add the currants and enough milk to bind.
3 Roll out ¼ inch thick and cut into rounds.
4 Cook in a thick based frying pan and serve hot with butter.

Queen cakes

cooking time 20 minutes

you will need:

6 oz. self-raising flour	2 eggs
good pinch salt	milk to mix
4 oz. butter or margarine	4 oz. currants
4 oz. castor sugar	

1 Sieve the flour and salt into a bowl.
2 Cream the fat and sugar until light in colour and fluffy in texture.
3 Beat the eggs lightly with a fork. Beat into the creamed fat folding in a little flour.
4 Stir in the milk. Fold in the remaining flour using a metal spoon and stir in the fruit.
5 Half fill paper baking cases (about 20) on a baking sheet, or greased patty tins.
6 Bake in a moderately hot oven on the middle shelf (375° F.—Gas Mark 5).
The flavour may be varied by adding 2–3 drops vanilla essence or grated lemon or orange rind, to the creamed fat.

Raisin cakes

cooking time 20 minutes

you will need:

8 oz. self-raising flour	4 oz. sugar
½ teaspoon salt	1 egg
3 oz. margarine	milk to mix
4 oz. raisins, roughly chopped	

1 Sieve flour and salt into a bowl.
2 Rub in fat. Add sugar and raisins.
3 Stir in egg, lightly beaten and milk to give a soft dropping consistency.
4 Half fill paper baking cases on a baking tray.
5 Bake in a hot oven (400° F.—Gas Mark 6), until golden.

Chocolate cakes

cooking time 15–20 minutes

you will need:

5 oz. self-raising flour	2 eggs
1 oz. cocoa	3–4 drops vanilla essence
good pinch salt	milk to mix
3 oz. butter or margarine	chocolate glacé icing (see
3 oz. sugar	page 64)

1 Sieve flour, cocoa and salt into a bowl.
2 Cream fat and sugar and add the essence.
3 Beat in the egg, folding in a little flour.
4 Fold in the remaining flour and lightly stir in the milk.
5 Three-quarters fill 12–15 paper baking cases and place on a baking sheet.
6 Bake on the middle shelf of a moderately hot oven (375° F.—Gas Mark 5).
Cool on a wire tray. When cold, top each with a teaspoon of chocolate glacé icing.

Mushroom cakes

Make cakes as above. Cut out centres with a small sharp pointed knife or apple corer, not quite through to the bottom. Fill the centre with vanilla cream and replace the top. Dust with icing sugar.

Butterfly cakes

Make cakes as above. When cool, cut off tops. Make a small hollow in the centre of each with a teaspoon. Place a good teaspoon lemon curd in the centre of each. Cut the tops in half and replace, rounded edges outwards, to resemble wings. Dust with icing sugar.

Apricot surprise cakes

Make cakes as above. Cut off tops and make a small hollow in each. Fill with a teaspoon apricot jam and a little chopped almond if liked. Replace lid.

Norfolk shortbreads

cooking time 15–20 minutes

you will need:

5 oz. flour	4 oz. butter or margarine
2 oz. fine semolina	2 oz. sugar
pinch salt	

1 Sieve flour, semolina and salt.
2 Cream butter and sugar until fluffy then stir in dry ingredients.
3 Knead together lightly, turn out on to a floured board and roll out to $\frac{1}{4}$ inch thick. Cut into rounds with a 2 inch biscuit cutter and prick with a fork.
4 Bake on lightly greased baking trays in a moderate oven (350° F.—Gas Mark 4) until pale golden in colour.
5 Sprinkle with castor sugar then cool on a wire tray.

Lemon shortbread crescents

Add the grated rind of 1 lemon to the creamed butter and sugar mixture. Cut into crescent shapes.

Almond shortbread triangles

Reduce flour to 4 oz. and add 2 oz. ground almonds and a few drops almond essence to the creamed butter and sugar mixture. Cut into triangles.

Chocolate shortbread fingers

Sift $\frac{1}{2}$ oz. cocoa powder with the dry ingredients and add a few drops of vanilla essence to the creamed butter and sugar mixture. Cut into fingers.

Almond twists

cooking time 10 minutes

you will need:

5 oz. plain flour	few drops almond essence
pinch salt	*topping:*
3 oz. butter	little beaten egg white
2 dessertspoons castor sugar	castor sugar
	chopped almonds
1 egg	(optional)

1 Sift flour with salt. Rub in butter lightly. Add sugar.
2 Stir in beaten egg and essence. Mix to a soft dough.
3 Divide dough into 9 equal portions. Roll each into a long 'sausage' about 7 inches long, on a lightly floured surface.
4 Curl each round into a 'pincurl' shape. Place on a baking sheet.
5 Brush the top of each with egg white and sprinkle with castor sugar and finely chopped blanched almonds if available.
6 Bake in a hot oven (400° F.—Gas Mark 6) until golden.
7 Leave on a wire tray to cool.

Lemon fingers

cooking time 20–25 minutes

you will need:

4 oz. luxury margarine	5 oz. plain flour
2 oz. castor sugar	lemon curd

1 Place the margarine and sugar in a mixing bowl.
2 Sieve the flour into the fat and sugar.
3 Beat all together until soft and creamy with a wooden spoon—about 2 minutes.
4 Spread mixture into a Swiss roll tin. Mark in lines across surface using the back of a fork.
5 Bake near the top of a moderate oven (350° F.—Gas Mark 4).
6 While hot cut into fingers and lift carefully on to a wire tray with a palette knife.
7 When cold, sandwich together with lemon curd and dust with icing sugar.

Press cookies

cooking time 15–20 minutes

you will need:

4 oz. butter	2 oz. cornflour
4 oz. sugar	1 egg
4 oz. self-raising flour	glacé cherries (optional)

1 Sieve the flour and cornflour.
2 Cream the fat and sugar. Beat in the egg.
3 Fold in the flour.
4 Put the mixture into a cookie press and pipe out on to a greased tray.
5 Bake in a moderate oven (350° F.—Gas Mark 4), until lightly coloured.
   The cookies may be decorated with a halved glacé cherry before baking, or when cold, sandwiched together with strawberry cream.

Strawberry cream

Cream 1 rounded tablespoon butter with 1 tablespoon strawberry jam. Gradually work in 6 oz. sieved icing sugar. Add a few drops red colouring if liked.

Macaroon pastries

cooking time 30 minutes

you will need:

4 oz. shortcrust pastry (see page 67)	1 oz. flour
	5 oz. castor sugar
Jam	2 egg whites
4 oz. ground almonds	

1 Line patty or boat shaped tins with pastry, put a little jam in the bottom of each.
2 Mix almonds, flour and sugar. Whisk egg whites until stiff.
3 Fold the dry ingredients into the egg whites. Spoon the mixture into the pastry cases. Cut small strips of remaining pastry and arrange two strips across each tart.
4 Bake in a hot oven (400° F.—Gas Mark 6). The crosses of pastry may be omitted and a halved blanched almond or glacé cherry pressed into the centre of each.

Chocolate almond pastries

Make as above omitting pastry crosses. Allow tarts to cool and coat each with chocolate glacé icing.

Cherry macaroon pastries

Make as above, putting a little chopped glacé or maraschino cherry in the bottom of each tart instead of jam. Coat finished tarts with lemon flavoured glacé icing.

Pineapple and mincemeat slices

Line a shallow oblong tin with shortcrust pastry. Crimp the edges and prick with a fork. Spread with mincemeat and cover with drained crushed pineapple. Cover with another piece of pastry and seal the edges. Brush with beaten egg and sprinkle with sugar. Bake in a hot oven (425° F.—Gas Mark 7). When cold cut into slices.

Jam and coconut slices

Make as above, spreading the pastry with raspberry jam mixed with an equal quantity of coconut.

Apricot almond slices

Make as above, spreading the pastry with apricot jam and sprinkling it with ground almonds.

Macaroon drops

Cut pastry into rounds with a 2-inch fluted cutter. Place on a baking sheet. Heap a little almond mixture on to each. Bake for about 20 minutes. Coat with icing when cold. Sprinkle with chopped toasted almonds or grated chocolate.

Chocolate fingers

you will need:

4 oz. biscuits	few drops vanilla essence
1 oz. castor sugar	½ oz. grated chocolate
1 heaped tablespoon syrup	½ tablespoon warm water
2 oz. butter	2 oz. sieved icing sugar
1½ tablespoons cocoa	chocolate vermicelli

1 Break the biscuits into small pieces.
2 Place the sugar, syrup and butter in a saucepan and stir over a low heat until sugar is dissolved.
3 Bring to the boil, remove from the heat and add the cocoa and vanilla essence.
4 Stir in the biscuits, mix well and press the mixture into a greased tin.
5 Melt the chocolate in the water in a bowl over boiling water.
6 Gradually add the icing sugar until the mixture is thick enough to coat the back of a spoon.
7 Pour over the mixture in the tin and decorate with chocolate vermicelli.
8 When set, cut into fingers.

Gingerbread

cooking time 1¼ hours

you will need:

10 oz. flour	3 oz. chopped crystallised
2 oz. cornflour	ginger
1 level teaspoon	2 oz. chopped candied peel
bicarbonate of soda	8 oz. treacle
1 level teaspoon mixed	¼ pint milk
spice	6 tablespoons corn oil
¼ oz. ground ginger	1 egg
4 oz. soft brown sugar	

1 Grease a tin 10 × 7 × 2 inches.
2 Sieve the flour, cornflour, bicarbonate of soda and spices into a mixing bowl.
3 Stir in the sugar, candied peel and crystallised ginger.
4 Warm the treacle over a gentle heat, stirring in the milk, oil and beaten egg with a wooden spoon.
5 Pour the treacle mixture into the dry ingredients.
6 Beat well and pour into the prepared tin.
7 Bake in a moderate oven (350° F.—Gas Mark 4).
8 Turn out on to a wire tray to cool.

9 Coat with white glacé icing flavoured with lemon juice if liked, and decorate with sliced ginger.

Golden cakes

cooking time 15–20 minutes

you will need:

4 oz. margarine	8 oz. plain flour
4 oz. sugar	½ teaspoon baking powder
3 eggs	pinch salt
3 tablespoons marmalade	lemon icing (see page 56)

1 Grease 18 queen cake or deep patty tins.
2 Sieve flour, baking powder and salt.
3 Cream fat and sugar.
4 Beat in the eggs one at a time, beating each in well, before adding the next.
5 Stir in the marmalade.
6 Fold in the dry ingredients.
7 Half fill prepared tins.
8 Bake at 375° F.—Gas Mark 5.
9 Cool on a wire tray. Top each with lemon icing.

Tyrolean coffee gâteau

cooking time 40 minutes

you will need:

6 oz. flour	2 tablespoons coffee
½ level teaspoon salt	essence
2 level teaspoons baking	little milk
powder	glazing syrup
5 oz. soft brown sugar	chopped nuts
3½ fluid oz. corn oil	¼ pint double cream
2 eggs	

1 Grease a tin approximately 8½ × 1½ inches and line the bottom with a piece of greased paper.
2 Sieve the dry ingredients into a bowl.
3 Whisk together the corn oil and egg yolks, and coffee essence made up to 3½ fluid oz. with milk. Add to the dry ingredients.
4 Beat well to form a smooth slack batter, then fold in the stiffly beaten egg whites.
5 Turn the mixture into the prepared tin and bake in a moderately hot oven (375° F. —Gas Mark 5). Turn out and leave until cold.
6 When the cake is cold, return it to the cake tin. Pour the hot glazing syrup over and leave overnight.
7 Turn the cake out on to a serving dish and spread with the cream, whisked until thick and flavoured with coffee essence. Decorate with chopped nuts.

Glazing syrup

Boil 4 oz. sugar and ¼ pint strong black coffee briskly for 5 minutes. Remove from the heat and stir in 2 tablespoons brandy.

Cake Icings

Glacé icing

you will need:

8 oz. icing sugar
2–3 tablespoons warm water

flavouring and colouring as liked

1 Sieve the icing sugar into a bowl, using a wooden spoon to press sugar through sieve, if necessary.
2 Add water gradually, beating well until icing is smooth and glossy, and of a good coating consistency, i.e. will coat the back of a spoon.
3 Add flavouring and colouring, and blend it well into the mixture.

If icing is required only for the top of the cake, it should be slightly thicker so that it can be spread out smoothly and be kept to the edge.

Quantities of icing to use

To cover the top of a 6-inch sponge use 4 oz. icing sugar; a 7-inch cake or sponge 6 oz.; an 8–9-inch sponge 8 oz. If covering top and sides use at least double quantities.

Royal icing

you will need:

1 lb. icing sugar
2 egg whites

1 teaspoon lemon juice
½ teaspoon glycerine

1 Leave the egg whites in a cold place overnight.
2 Sieve the icing sugar.
3 Whisk the egg whites until frothy.
4 Beat in half the icing sugar, add the lemon juice and glycerine.
5 Continue beating in the sugar, until the icing can be drawn into stiff peaks.
6 Scrape the icing down from the sides of the bowl. Cover with a damp cloth and use as required.

Cake Fillings

Mock cream

you will need:

2 oz. butter
2 oz. castor sugar
1 tablespoon cold milk

1½ tablespoons boiling water

1 Cream the butter and sugar until light in colour and shiny.
2 Beat in the boiling water, a drop at a time.
3 Gradually add the milk in the same way.
4 Leave in a cold place until firm.

Continental cream

you will need:

¼ pint thick cream
1 egg yolk

bare 1 oz. icing sugar
¼ teaspoon vanilla essence

1 Sieve the icing sugar.
2 Whisk the cream until thick.
3 Beat the egg yolk with the sugar, adding the vanilla essence.
4 Fold the yolk mixture into the cream, mixing thoroughly.

Butter cream

you will need:

6–8 oz. icing sugar
4 oz. butter

vanilla essence

1 Sieve the icing sugar.
2 Beat butter with a wooden spoon or spatula until soft.
3 Beat icing sugar into the butter, adding a few drops of vanilla essence. The amount of icing sugar needed will depend on the consistency of the cream required.

Entertaining

Even if you have only the smallest 'bed-sitter' you will want to entertain occasionally, and it is great fun to do so.

Sandwiches, cake and coffee, or a salad are all acceptable, and in this chapter you will find simple recipes that are still rather special so that you can give your guests a genuine treat. And with careful planning, you can be even more ambitious.

The following dishes have been specially chosen so that they can be prepared, in most cases, without an oven, and with the minimum of equipment. You may have to borrow plates and cutlery, but don't forget that cardboard plates or waxed cartons can be used for the sweet or salad.

A paper 'table cloth' with matching serviettes will save on the laundry bill.

Appetisers

Grapefruit cocktail
you will need:

2 grapefruits	2 tablespoons sherry
2 oz. sugar	4 maraschino cherries
3 tablespoons boiling water	

1 Halve the grapefruit and remove the sections of flesh.
2 Dissolve the sugar in the water, add the sherry and pour over the fruit.
3 Cover, and chill in a refrigerator if possible, until ready to serve.
4 Spoon into sundae glasses and decorate with cherries.

Tomato juice cocktail
you will need:

1 15-oz. can tomato juice	1 teaspoon Worcester-
1 tablespoon lemon juice	shire sauce
1 teaspoon mint vinegar	little sugar
salt and freshly ground pepper	

1 Blend all the ingredients together, seasoning to taste.
2 Chill if possible and stir before serving.

Coral cocktail
you will need:

few mint leaves	$\frac{1}{4}$ pint fresh orange juice
1 15-oz. can tomato juice	sugar and salt

1 Bruise the mint leaves and pour the tomato juice on to them.
2 Add the orange juice and season to taste with sugar and salt.

3 Serve very cold in tall narrow glasses, garnished with a very thin slice of orange.

Stuffed tomatoes
cooking time 20 minutes
you will need:

4 large tomatoes	2 rashers streaky bacon
pinch salt, pepper and sugar	2 oz. grated cheese
4 round fried bread	

1 Cut a slice from the top of each tomato, scoop out the pulp.
2 Sprinkle the inside of each with salt, pepper and sugar.
3 Chop the bacon and fry for 2–3 minutes, mix with tomato pulp, cheese and breadcrumbs.
4 Fill the tomatoes with this mixture and replace the tops.
5 Bake in a moderate oven (350° F.—Gas Mark 4).
6 Serve on rounds of fried bread.

Californian salad
you will need:

4 pineapple rings	2 oz. walnuts, chopped
6–8 oz. cream cheese	lettuce

1 Arrange crisp lettuce leaves on 4 individual plates.
2 Place a pineapple ring on each and top with a small round of cream cheese.
3 Sprinkle with chopped walnuts and serve.
Alternatively, place 2–3 cooked prunes in the centre of each pineapple ring and top with a spoonful of cream cheese.

Stuffed ham rolls

you will need:

8 thin slices cooked ham
16 sprigs watercress
mild mustard
1 packet frozen mixed
   vegetables
mayonnaise (see page 71)

1 Prepare vegetables in mayonnaise as for Russian eggs.
2 Spread thin slices of ham with a little mild mustard.
3 Place a spoonful of vegetables on each, roll up and tuck a sprig of watercress into the end of each.
4 Alternatively, stuff ham with cream cheese mixed with grated apple and sultanas.

Spanish hors-d'oeuvre

you will need:

1 large Spanish onion
1 cucumber
6 tomatoes
seasoning
6 stoned olives
French dressing (see
   page 70)
2 tablespoons grated
   Parmesan cheese

1 Slice the onion very thinly.
2 Cut the cucumber into thin slices and the tomatoes into thicker slices.
3 Arrange in a bowl in layers, seasoning each layer with salt and pepper and sprinkling with French dressing and the grated cheese.
4 Garnish with olives.

Russian eggs

you will need:

4 eggs
mayonnaise (see page 71)
paprika pepper or sliced
   olives to garnish
1 packet frozen mixed
   vegetables

1 Hard-boil eggs, cut in half lengthwise.
2 Cook frozen mixed vegetables, drain and mix with mayonnaise.
3 Place two heaped tablespoons vegetables on each plate, place two pieces of egg on each.
4 Coat eggs with mayonnaise and dust with paprika pepper or garnish with sliced olives.

Quick cream of chicken soup

cooking time 20–25 minutes

you will need:

1 oz. butter
1 oz. flour
$\frac{3}{4}$ pint chicken stock
$\frac{1}{4}$ pint milk
salt and pepper
nutmeg
4–6 oz. cooked chicken
2 tablespoons cream

1 Melt the butter and stir in the flour, cook over a gentle heat for 3 minutes.
2 Gradually add stock, then milk, stirring well throughout, bring to the boil.
3 Season with salt, pepper and a little freshly grated nutmeg, add chicken, minced or chopped, and cook gently for 10–15 minutes.
4 Stir in cream and serve.

Two's company

Corn chowder

cooking time 12–15 minutes

you will need:

1 rasher fat bacon, chopped
1 small onion, chopped
8 oz. potatoes, peeled and
   diced
$\frac{1}{4}$ pint boiling water
1 small packet frozen
   sweet corn
1 tomato, chopped
seasoning
$\frac{1}{2}$ pint milk

1 Fry the bacon until crisp, remove from the pan.
2 Add the onion to the pan and fry until soft.
3 Add the potatoes and boiling water, cover and boil for about 10 minutes.
4 Add the corn and the tomato, bring to the boil and boil for 2 minutes.
5 Add the milk, bacon and salt and pepper to taste.
6 Stir well, reheat gently and serve at once.

Devilled omelette

you will need:

3 eggs
good pinch salt
pinch cayenne pepper or
   sprinkling white pepper
$\frac{1}{4}$ level teaspoon dry
   mustard
good pinch curry powder
1 carton cultured cream or
   single cream with
   1 dessertspoon lemon
   juice
1 tablespoon water
4 oz. chopped ham
good $\frac{1}{2}$ oz. butter

1 Whisk together the eggs, seasoning, half the cream, water and half the ham.
2 Melt the butter in a pan and pour in the mixture.
3 Cook gently, stirring occasionally and loosening the edges until golden underneath and lightly set.
4 Brown the top lightly under the grill.
5 Top with remaining cream and sprinkle with the rest of the ham.
6 Serve with a green salad.

Grilled chicken—country style

cooking time 30 minutes

you will need:

2 small chicken halves	2 rashers streaky bacon
$\frac{1}{2}$ lemon	2 oz. mushrooms
1$\frac{1}{2}$ oz. butter	watercress
salt	potato crisps

Skewer each chicken half as flat as possible and rub over with cut lemon.

Melt the butter and brush liberally all over the chicken.

Sprinkle with salt.

Remove the rack from the grill pan and lay the halves skin side down in the pan.

Place the pan 5–6 inches below a medium heat grill, and grill the chicken for 10–12 minutes.

Turn the chicken over, brush with more butter and continue grilling for a further 12–15 minutes, brushing with butter once or twice.

When cooked, the chicken skin should be crisp and golden brown.

Meanwhile, cut the bacon into strips and slice the mushrooms. Fry in the remaining butter and when cooked, add the lemon juice.

Pour the dressing over the chicken and serve garnished with watercress and potato crisps.

Pineapple chicken grill

cooking time 30 minutes

you will need:

2 small chicken halves	2 oz. butter
1 small can pineapple	salt
cubes	few sprigs fresh mint—if
1 tablespoon lemon juice	available

Drain the syrup from the pineapple cubes, add the lemon juice and pour over the chicken. Leave to soak for 1 hour.

Melt the butter in a small pan.

Drain and dry the chicken then brush liberally with butter on both sides and sprinkle with salt.

Remove the rack from the grill pan and arrange the chicken skin side down in the pan.

Place the pan 5–6 inches below the source of heat and grill gently for 10–12 minutes.

Turn the chicken over, brush with butter and continue grilling gently for 12–15 minutes, brushing occasionally with butter.

Meanwhile, add the drained and dried pineapple cubes to the remaining butter and toss together over a gentle heat for a few minutes.

Serve the chicken halves on a flat dish with the pineapple cubes sprinkled with finely chopped mint between them.

Garnish with sprigs of mint.

Spaghetti with sauce

cooking time about 30 minutes

you will need:

6 oz. long spaghetti	2 large tomatoes, cut in
salt and pepper	quarters
1 oz. cooking fat	1 tablespoon tomato purée
8 oz. skinless pork sausages	1 teaspoon Worcester-
1 large onion, finely	shire sauce
chopped	1 oz. plain flour
2 oz. grated cheese	

1 Cook the spaghetti in boiling salted water until tender—about 20 minutes.
2 Make the sauce as described below.
3 Melt the fat, add the halved sausages and cook for 5 minutes turning frequently.
4 Add the onion and fry gently until soft. Remove pan from the heat.
5 Add the tomatoes, tomato purée and Worcestershire sauce. Season to taste with salt and pepper.
6 Mix the flour to a smooth paste with a little cold water. Gradually add $\frac{1}{2}$ pint water. Add to the saucepan and bring to the boil stirring all the time until thickened.
7 Cook gently for 15 minutes.
8 Drain the spaghetti and arrange on a hot dish. Pour the sauce over the spaghetti, sprinkle with cheese and serve at once.

Liver risotto

cooking time 25–30 minutes

you will need:

2 oz. fat	$\frac{1}{2}$ oz. butter
3 oz. onion	4 oz. liver
6 oz. Patna rice	2 oz. cooked, sweet red
2 beef extract cubes	pepper
1 pint hot water	salt and pepper
1 oz. bacon	grated cheese

1 Peel and chop the onion. Wash the liver in warm water, drain and dry. Cut into small pieces.
2 Remove the rind from the bacon and chop. Slice the pepper.
3 Heat the fat in a pan and fry the onion until brown. Add the rice and cook for a further 3 minutes.
4 Add a quarter of the stock (made by pouring the boiling water on to the beef cubes) and boil gently adding more stock as required.
5 Cook for 15–20 minutes until the rice is cooked and the stock absorbed.
6 Meanwhile, fry the bacon in the butter and then fry the liver lightly.
7 Add to the cooked rice with the red pepper and heat well. Season to taste and serve at once with grated cheese served separately.

Shrimp pancakes

cooking time 20 minutes

you will need:

3½ oz. plain flour	*stuffing:*
1 oz. quick breakfast oats	½ pint white sauce (see
½ pint milk	page 68)
1 egg	1 small carton shrimps
¼ teaspoon salt	lemon juice
2 oz. fat for frying	salt to taste
cayenne pepper	
pink colouring	

1 Mix the flour, oats and salt together in a bowl.

2 Add the egg and gradually beat in the milk. Allow to stand for 1 hour.

3 Add lemon juice, salt and pepper to taste to the white sauce. Add a little colouring to tint the sauce pink.

4 Add the shrimps to the sauce, reheat if necessary.

5 Cook the pancakes in a little very hot fat for about 3 minutes on each side. To keep pancakes hot, place in a soup plate over a pan of boiling water, cover with pan lid.

6 Fill each pancake with shrimp stuffing and serve very hot.

Four for a meal

Company casserole

cooking time about 45 minutes

you will need:

1 small onion	1 tablespoon sherry
1 oz. butter	(optional)
½ packet (3 tablespoons)	4 slices ham
dried tomato soup	½ can sweet corn niblets

1 Peel and chop onion, fry in melted butter for 5 minutes.

2 Blend in soup and cook for a further 3 minutes.

3 Gradually stir in ½ pint water and bring to boil.

4 Heap a tablespoon of sweet corn on each slice of ham, roll ham up and place in bottom of a greased ovenproof dish.

5 Add sherry, if used, to sauce, pour over ham.

6 Cover and bake in a moderate oven (350° F.—Gas Mark 4), for 30 minutes.

7 Serve with thick slices of French bread or garlic bread (see below) or potato crisps heated through in the oven.

Note:

The ham and corn may be cooked in the sauce if an oven is not available. Cover and simmer gently for 20 minutes. This recipe may be varied using canned celery hearts in place of sweet corn and a cheese sauce. Pour cheese sauce over the ham, bake in a moderately hot oven for 30 minutes.

Garlic bread

cooking time 15 minutes

you will need:

1 clove garlic	1 French or Vienna loaf
2 oz. butter	

1 Chop garlic finely.

2 Cream butter with a wooden spoon blending in garlic.

3 Cut loaf into thick slices, spread with butter.

4 Bake in a moderate oven (350° F.—Gas Mark 4), for 15 minutes or toast under a hot grill. Serve as an accompaniment to vegetable soup.

Spaghetti alla Bolognese

cooking time just over 1 hour

you will need:

1 lb. spaghetti	1 strip lemon peel
2 tablespoons butter	1 bay leaf
4 tablespoons oil	4 tablespoons tomato
8 oz. green bacon, finely	purée
chopped	½ pint beef stock
1 onion, finely chopped	¼ pint dry white wine
2 carrots, finely chopped	salt, pepper, grated nutmeg
1 stick celery, finely	4 tablespoons cream
chopped	freshly grated Parmesan
8 oz. sirloin of beef, minced	cheese

1 Heat the butter and oil in a large thick bottomed pan.

2 Add the bacon, onion, carrots and celery and sauté over a medium heat, stirring occasionally, for a few minutes.

3 Stir in the beef and stir until browned evenly.

4 Add the lemon peel, bay leaf, tomato purée, stock, wine, salt, pepper and nutmeg to taste.

5 Cover the pan and simmer for 30 minutes, stirring occasionally.

6 Remove the lemon peel and bay leaf and simmer uncovered for a further 30 minutes until the sauce has thickened slightly.

7 Add the cream and simmer for 2–3 minutes.

8 Meanwhile cook the spaghetti in boiling salted water until just tender. Drain and serve with the Bolognese sauce poured over and the cheese served separately.

Tarragon lamb

cooking time 1½–2 hours

you will need:

1½ lb. middle neck of lamb	1 oz. butter or margarine
½ pint water	1 oz. flour
1 level teaspoon dried	3 tablespoons white wine
tarragon	¼ pint sour cream or
1 level teaspoon salt	yoghourt
ground pepper	chopped chives
1 small onion, sliced	

Cut meat into pieces and simmer gently in the water with the tarragon, salt, freshly ground pepper and onion.

When tender, drain the meat from the liquor. Remove bones and place the meat on a serving dish.

Melt the butter or margarine, add the flour and cook 2 minutes.

Gradually add the liquor and the wine, stirring all the time.

Bring to the boil and boil for 5 minutes.

Add the sour cream or yoghourt and re-season with salt and pepper.

Re-heat without boiling and pour over the meat.

Garnish with chopped chives and serve.

Uncle Sam's fried chicken

cooking time 25–30 minutes

you will need:

4–8 chicken joints as	¼ level teaspoon pepper
required	*garnish:*
2 rounded tablespoons flour	watercress (optional)
1 level teaspoon salt	potato crisps

Put the flour and seasoning into a stout paper bag and add the joints two at a time and shake until evenly coated with flour.

Melt enough fat to give ½ inch depth in a strong pan.

When the fat is hot, add the joints and fry until lightly browned, turning once or twice—about 10 minutes.

Reduce the heat, cover the pan tightly and continue cooking a further 15 minutes until the chicken is tender.

Remove the lid for the last 5 minutes cooking to allow the skin to crisp. Drain well.

Arrange the chicken on a hot dish and garnish with watercress or leave on kitchen paper until cold for 'finger eating'. Serve with potato crisps.

Wellington lamb

cooking time about 2 hours

you will need:

large boned breast of lamb	6 oz. rice
1 oz. cooking fat	1 large packet frozen peas
12 oz. onions, thinly sliced	4 oz. large sliced
8 oz. diced carrots	mushrooms or whole
1 pint stock or water	button ones
salt and pepper	¼ pint red wine

1 Cut the lamb into pieces and brown in the melted fat with the onions.
2 Add the carrots, stock or water, and seasoning.
3 Cover and cook over a low heat for about 1½ hours until tender.
4 Add the rice and 10 minutes later add the peas, mushrooms and wine.
5 Cover again and simmer until the vegetables are cooked—about 30 minutes.
6 Stir occasionally and if the rice should stick, add a little hot water, or stock.

Poulet cocotte bonne femme

cooking time about 1¾ hours

you will need:

3–3½ lb. chicken	4 oz. sausage meat
salt and pepper	1 tablespoon fresh
2½ oz. butter	breadcrumbs
4 oz. lean bacon, cut into	1 chicken liver, chopped
dice	1 tablespoon chopped
1 lb. potatoes, cut into	parsley
⅓-inch cubes	parsley or chives for
	seasoning

1 Remove the giblets and season the chicken inside and out with salt and pepper.
2 Mix the sausage meat, breadcrumbs, liver and parsley together and use to stuff into the neck end of the bird.
3 Replace the flap of skin and secure under the wing tips.
4 Melt the butter in a large heavy based casserole, and lightly brown the chicken all over.
5 Add the bacon, cover and cook gently for 15 minutes.
6 Baste the chicken, add the potatoes, turning them over in the fat. Replace the lid and continue cooking over a gentle heat for about 1½ hours, until tender.
7 Serve in the casserole, sprinkling the potatoes with a little chopped parsley or chives.

Note:

If a casserole with a heavy base is not available, the chicken can be cooked in a large saucepan with a well-fitting lid.

Steak and mushroom kebabs

cooking time about 20 minutes

you will need:

1 lb. steak	2 tablespoons tomato
12 small mushrooms	ketchup
¼ pint red wine	1 level teaspoon sugar
¼ pint corn oil	½ level teaspoon salt
1 teaspoon Worcestershire	1 tablespoon vinegar
sauce	pinch dried marjoram
1 clove garlic, chopped	pinch dried rosemary
fine	

1 Cut the steak in small cubes and peel and stalk the mushrooms.
2 Mix all the other ingredients together in a basin and add the steak and mushrooms.
3 Leave to marinate for 2 hours, then alternate steak squares and mushrooms on skewers and grill until tender, basting frequently with the marinade.
4 Serve with boiled rice.

Devilled fish salad

you will need:

8 oz. canned tuna or salmon	1 teaspoon curry powder
or freshly cooked fish	1 tablespoon lemon juice
1 can celery hearts	or vinegar
2 tablespoons chopped	12 oz. cold cooked rice
unpeeled cucumber	about 2½ tablespoons oil
3 tablespoons mayonnaise	and vinegar dressing
or salad cream (see	1 tablespoon chopped
page 71)	parsley
1 tablespoon French or	
mild mustard	

1 Chill the fish and celery hearts.
2 Just before serving, flake the fish and slice the drained celery. Mix lightly with the cucumber.
3 Blend the mayonnaise, mustard, curry powder and lemon juice.
4 Toss the rice with the dressing and parsley.
5 Spoon the rice on to a serving plate, heap the fish salad on top and spoon the mayonnaise over the top.
6 If liked, garnish with sliced hard-boiled egg or a few strips of sweet red pepper.

Desserts and teatime cookery

Orange cream pie

cooking time about 10 minutes

you will need:

6 oz. sweet meal biscuits	1 small can evaporated milk
3 oz. butter, melted	2 teaspoons lemon juice
½ orange jelly	grated chocolate
1 can mandarin oranges	(optional)

1 Put the biscuits between two sheets of grease-proof paper or foil.
2 Roll with a rolling pin until the biscuits are crushed into fine crumbs.
3 Put the crumbs into a bowl, stir in the butter and mix well.
4 Brush an 8-inch pie plate with melted butter. Press the crumb mixture over the bottom and sides of the plate. Leave in a cold place to set.
5 Drain the juice from the mandarin oranges. Measure ¼ pint of the juice and bring to the boil in a small pan.
6 Pour the juice on to the jelly and stir until the jelly is dissolved. Leave in a cool place until thick.
7 Meanwhile pour the milk into a basin, add the lemon juice and whisk until thick.
8 Whisk the milk into the jelly and continue whisking until the mixture is thick and fluffy.

9 Chop half the mandarin oranges, stir into the jelly mixture and pile into the prepared case.
10 Leave to set. Decorate with remaining mandarin oranges and sprinkle with grated chocolate if liked.

Lemon cream pie

you will need:

6 oz. sweet meal biscuits	1 small can evaporated
3 oz. butter melted	milk
1 lemon jelly	grated rind and juice 1
boiling water	lemon
	milk chocolate flake

1 Prepare the biscuit crust as for orange cream pie.
2 Dissolve the jelly in a little hot water and make up to ½ pint with cold water. Leave in a cool place until thick and just about to set.
3 Whisk the milk with the lemon juice and rind until thick.
4 Whisk the milk into the jelly and pour into the prepared case.
5 Leave in a cold place to set. When set, decorate with crumbled chocolate flake.

Tipsy cake

cooking time about 35 minutes

you will need:

1 sponge cake (see page 49)	blanched almonds
raspberry jam	angelica
¼ pint sherry or Madeira	glacé cherries
1 pint custard (see page 42)	

Make sponge cake.

Prepare custard.

Split the sponge cake and spread thickly with jam.

Sandwich together again and place in a dish.

Pour the wine over the cake and leave to soak for 1 hour.

Pour the custard over the cake and stick blanched almonds into it to resemble a porcupine. Decorate with cherries and angelica.

Raspberry gâteau

cooking time 25 minutes

you will need:

2 8-inch rounds sponge or	¼ pint double cream
sandwich cake (see	thick white glacé icing
page 49)	lemon flavoured (see
8 oz. raspberries	page 56)
2 oz. castor sugar	

Make sponge.

Mash half the raspberries with the castor sugar. Spread over one cake, top with cream, whisked until thick, and cover with a second round of cake.

Coat with thick glacé icing and decorate with remaining raspberries.

Serve as soon as the icing is set.

Mandarin gâteau

Make as above, using drained mandarin oranges in place of the raspberries and omitting the castor sugar. Sprinkle the icing with coarsely grated chocolate and decorate with mandarins.

Strawberry meringue gâteau

Make as above, using strawberries instead of raspberries, piling more whipped cream with the strawberries on top of the cake. Decorate with small whole meringues or pieces of meringue.

Pear delice

you will need:

4 pear halves	¼ pint chocolate sauce
1 family brick strawberry	(see page 70)
ice cream	1 oz. plain chocolate

1 Place a pear half in 4 individual dishes, hollow side up.

2 Place a slice or scoop of ice cream on each pear and coat with hot chocolate sauce.

3 Sprinkle with grated chocolate and serve at once.

Ice cream with hot fruit and rum topping

you will need:

1 tablespoon sugar	1 teaspoon arrowroot
¼ pint water	3 glacé cherries, quartered
4 oz. seeded raisins	vanilla ice cream
1 tablespoon rum or rum	whole blanched almonds
essence to taste	(optional)

1 Dissolve the sugar in the water and boil until syrupy.

2 Add the raisins and simmer very gently for a few minutes.

3 Remove the raisins to a plate.

4 Mix the arrowroot with a little cold water and use to thicken the syrup.

5 Allow to cool for 5 minutes, then stir in the raisins, rum or rum essence, and the cherries.

6 Pour over portions of ice cream and, if liked, decorate with whole blanched almonds.

Jellied fruit flan

you will need:

pastry (see page 67)	canned fruit
¼ pint fruit juice	2 teaspoons powdered
sugar to taste	gelatine

1 Fill a cooked pastry flan case with drained fruit.

2 Heat fruit juice in a small pan, stir in powdered gelatine.

3 Heat gently until the gelatine dissolves.

4 Add sugar to taste.

5 Leave in a cool place until just about to set.

6 Spoon over the fruit and leave until completely set.

7 Serve with cream.

Whipped cream

you will need:

1 dessertspoon sherry	1½ oz. castor sugar
1 dessertspoon brandy (optional)	½ pint double cream
rind and juice ½ lemon	

1 Put the sherry, brandy if used, lemon juice and rind (finely grated), and the sugar into a bowl.
2 Stir until the sugar is dissolved.
3 Add the cream, stir well in and whisk until the mixture is thick.

Chocolate cake

cooking time about 25 minutes

you will need:

	filling:
4 oz. luxury margarine	
5 oz. castor sugar	2 oz. plain chocolate
4 oz. self-raising flour	2 oz. luxury margarine
1 heaped tablespoon cocoa	1 oz. castor sugar
2 eggs	1 dessertspoon hot water
1 tablespoon milk	1 dessertspoon milk
chocolate icing (see below) or castor sugar	1–2 drops flavouring essence (optional)

1 Grease two 7-inch sandwich tins and line the bottom with greaseproof paper.
2 Put margarine and sugar in a mixing bowl. Sieve in flour and cocoa.
3 Add milk and eggs and beat all ingredients together with a wooden spoon for 2 minutes.
4 Divide the mixture between the tins and smooth the top.
5 Bake in the middle of a moderate oven (350° F.—Gas Mark 4), for 20–25 minutes.
6 Turn on to a wire tray to cool. When the cakes are cold, sandwich together with the filling and coat the top with chocolate icing or sprinkle with castor sugar.

To make the filling

1 Melt the chocolate in a basin over hot water.
2 Allow the chocolate to cool and whisk it together with the margarine and sugar until light and fluffy.
3 Add the water, milk and 1–2 drops of flavouring.
4 Whisk again and use.
   For a 'special' cake, make double the quantity of filling and use half of it as a frosty topping using a small palette knife or fork to swirl a design on the top before the filling sets.

To make chocolate icing

Add a few drops of water and olive oil to melted chocolate. Or make a coating icing by blending 2 oz. melted chocolate with 4 oz. icing sugar and 1 tablespoon water. A few drops of oil can be added for extra gloss.

Almond cherry desserts

you will need:

3 oz. blanched almonds	¼ pint syrup from the cherries
oil for frying	
3 oz. maraschino cherries	vanilla ice cream

1 Halve the almonds and fry them in olive oil until golden brown.
2 Drain them well and place in a bowl with the halved cherries and the syrup.
3 Arrange alternate layers of the cherry mixture and vanilla ice cream in individual tall glasses. Finish with a layer of cherry and almond.

Vanilla and chocolate sundae

you will need:

1 small brick vanilla ice cream	2 oz. chopped walnuts
	¼ pint cream
1 small brick chocolate ice cream	maraschino cherries
½ pint chocolate sauce (see page 70)	

1 Place a scoop of chocolate ice cream in individual dishes.
2 Coat with chocolate sauce and top each with a scoop vanilla ice cream. Coat again with chocolate sauce.
3 Sprinkle with chopped nuts and pipe with whipped cream, sweetened to taste.
4 Decorate with cherries and serve at once.

Ring doughnuts

cooking time 5–8 minutes

you will need:

6 oz. self-raising flour	2½ tablespoons milk
½ level teaspoon mixed spice	2 oz. castor sugar
	pinch salt
1 tablespoon blended vegetable oil	oil for frying
	1 egg

Sieve flour, spice and salt into a bowl. Add the sugar.

Beat the tablespoon oil, egg and milk together. Stir into the dry ingredients and mix to a soft dough.

Turn dough on to a floured surface. Roll out $\frac{1}{4}$ inch thick.

Cut into rounds with a 3-inch cutter. Cut out centres, forming rings with a $1\frac{1}{2}$-inch cutter.

Re-roll remaining pieces of dough.

Pour enough oil into a deep frying pan to fill it $\frac{1}{3}$ full.

Heat oil to 365° F. (a cube of bread will become golden on one side in 30 seconds).

Fry doughnuts one at a time until golden, turning them frequently during cooking.

Remove from oil with a perforated spoon, leave on crumpled kitchen paper to drain.

Toss in castor sugar. Serve on a doyley. Makes 12.

Iced rings

Make as above, when cold spoon thin white glacé icing (vanilla or lemon flavoured) over the rings. Serve when the icing has set.

Cinnamon rings

Make as above, omitting mixed spice. Toss rings in castor sugar mixed with powdered cinnamon.

Neapolitan sandwiches

1 Prepare thin bread and butter, both brown and white.
2 Prepare three or four savoury fillings of contrasting colours, e.g. tomato, liver pâté, watercress and egg.
3 Spread a piece of the bread and butter with one of the fillings and cover with a second piece of bread, buttered side down.
4 Now butter the top, spread with one of the other fillings and cover with a third piece of bread and butter.
5 Continue in this way, building up a large block of alternate layers of bread, butter and filling, working the different colours in rotation.
6 Cut off the crust and press well.
7 Wrap the whole block in foil or waxed paper and leave in a cool place for some hours with a weight on top.
8 When required, cut into slices across the filling, making sandwiches of many colour stripes.
9 Arrange the sandwiches on a plate to show the striped effect.

Drinks

Coffee 'night cap'
you will need:
1 tablespoon instant coffee 1 tablespoon brown sugar
1 tablespoon boiling water bare $\frac{1}{2}$ pint milk

Dissolve coffee in water, add sugar.
Stir in the milk, bring just to the boil.
Serve at once.

Iced coffee
you will need:

2 heaped tablespoons	$\frac{1}{4}$ pint milk
instant coffee	ice cubes
1 tablespoon hot water	ice cream or fresh cream
1 dessertspoon sugar	(optional)

Dissolve coffee in hot water, add sugar.
Stir in milk and add enough ice cubes to make up to $\frac{1}{2}$ pint.

3 Serve in a tall glass topped with a spoonful of ice cream or cream, if liked.

Iced tea
you will need:

1 pint weak tea	1 thin slice lemon
sugar to taste	few cloves or mint leaves
1 thin slice orange	ice cubes

1 Strain tea, add sugar to taste.
2 Place slice of orange and lemon, studded with cloves, if used, in a jug.
3 Pour on tea, add two or three ice cubes and serve. Mint leaves may be added with ice, if cloves are not used. This is enough for two people.

Spanish punch

cooking time about 10 minutes

you will need:

4 oz. raisins	1 pint water
juice and rind ½ lemon	½ glass sherry

1 Chop raisins, add lemon rind and simmer in water until liquid is reduced to ½ pint.
2 Strain, add lemon juice and sherry.
3 Serve hot. This amount is enough for two glasses.

Peach cream shake

you will need:

4 tablespoons peach purée	½ pint milk
pinch salt	1 heaped tablespoon ice
2–3 drops almond essence	cream

1 To make purée, finely chop or sieve canned peaches.
2 Add salt and almond essence.
3 Gradually whisk in milk.
4 Stir or whisk in ice cream.
5 Serve at once. This amount is enough for two glasses.

Blackcurrant refresher

you will need:

1 tablespoon blackcurrant	½ pint boiling water
jam	castor sugar
1 teaspoon lemon juice	

1 Blend jam and lemon juice.
2 Pour on boiling water, stirring.
3 Add about 1 teaspoon sugar if required.
4 Leave until cold, strain and serve.

Lemon soda

you will need:

juice 1 large lemon	1 small bottle soda water
castor sugar to taste	mint leaves if available

1 Squeeze the juice from lemon, strain into a tumbler.
2 Add 1 teaspoon sugar, stir until dissolved.
3 Pour on soda water, stir well.
4 Add more sugar, to taste.
5 Garnish with 2 or 3 mint leaves if available.
6 Serve at once.

Banana milk shake

you will need:

1 ripe banana	sugar
½ pint milk	cinnamon (optional)

1 Peel and slice the banana into a basin.
2 Mash and whisk with a fork until smooth.
3 Gradually whisk in milk.
4 Add sugar to taste.
5 Add a pinch of cinnamon if liked and serve.

Lemon honey drink

you will need:

juice 1 lemon	about ¼ pint boiling water
1 heaped tablespoon honey	

1 Squeeze and strain the juice from the lemon.
2 Blend with honey.
3 Gradually stir in boiling water and serve.

Basic recipes for reference

Making coffee

The jug method is the easiest and one of the best methods.
For every pint of water, you need 2 heaped tablespoons coffee (fine ground).
1 Heat jug by filling it with boiling water and allowing it to stand about 5 minutes.
2 Empty jug and dry it.
3 Put coffee in the jug and pour on the boiling water, stirring vigorously.
4 Leave jug in a warm place for 5 minutes, stirring once or twice.
5 Leave without stirring for a further 5 minutes. The coffee is then ready to serve. If there appears to be too many grounds on the top, lightly skim these off with a spoon or carefully pour off one cup of coffee and then pour back into jug. This will cause the grounds to settle. If you are serving the coffee in another pot, make sure that the pot is really hot. If it is necessary to reheat the coffee, take care that it does not boil.
Serve with warm milk or thin cream.

Shortcrust pastry

you will need:

8 oz. flour	2 oz. lard (or cooking fat)
pinch salt	cold water to mix
2 oz. margarine	

Sieve the flour and salt into a mixing bowl. Chop the fat roughly and add to the flour. Rub the fat into the flour, using the finger tips, until the mixture resembles breadcrumbs. Add cold water gradually and knead the mixture lightly by hand until it works together into a firm dough.

Turn out on to a lightly floured surface and knead lightly until smooth. Turn pastry over and roll out as required.

To make a flan case

Make shortcrust pastry.

Roll out pastry into a circle about 2 inches larger than the flan ring.

Place flan ring on a baking sheet. Place the round of pastry over the ring and press into shape, taking care that the pastry fits well against the inside edge, but that it is not stretched.

Trim off surplus pastry, by passing the rolling pin over the edge of the ring. Place a piece of lightly greased greaseproof, greased side down, in the flan and fill the flan with uncooked rice, haricot beans or macaroni.

Bake in a hot oven (400° F.—Gas Mark 6) until the pastry is firm—15 minutes. Pastry baked in this way is described as 'baked blind'. This is done to ensure a good shape. The rice, etc., can be stored in a jar and used indefinitely for the purpose.

Remove filling and paper from flan. Return flan to oven for a further five minutes to allow base to cook through.

Remove flan ring and leave flan case on a wire tray until cold. Cold cooked pastry may be stored in an air-tight tin and used as required.

Note:

If a flan ring is not available, a sandwich tin may be used but strips of strong paper should be placed across the inside of the tin to protrude at the edges before the pastry is fitted. This will enable the flan case to be removed easily from the tin after cooking.

Tartlets

Make 3 oz. shortcrust pastry (see top left). Roll out thinly and cut into rounds with a fluted cutter (a little larger than the patty tins being used). Line 6 patty tins with the pastry, pressing it well with the fingers.

Jam or lemon curd tartlets

Half-fill each with jam or lemon curd and bake in a hot oven (400° F.—Gas Mark 6) for 15–20 minutes.

Syrup tartlets

Half-fill with a mixture of 2 large tablespoons warmed syrup, 2 tablespoons cake or breadcrumbs and the juice ½ lemon. Bake as above.

Individual fruit pie

Use an aluminium foil patty pan or pie dish about 4½-inch size and allow 2 oz. shortcrust pastry and 3 heaped tablespoons stewed, sweetened fruit for each. Roll out the pastry and cut out a round to fit the pan and 1 round slightly smaller for the top. Line the pan, fill with fruit and damp the edges of the pastry. Put on pastry lid, pinch edges together and flute. Brush with milk and sprinkle with sugar. Make a small slit in the top, bake in a hot oven (400° F.—Gas Mark 6) for about 20 minutes. Serve hot or cold.

Savoury pies

These can be made in the same way.

Suet pastry

you will need:

4 oz. flour (with plain flour use ½ teaspoon baking powder)	2 oz. shredded suet
	pinch salt
	water to mix

1 Sieve flour and salt and baking powder—if used.

2 Add suet and mix in using a long-bladed knife.

3 Stir in enough water to make a firm dough.

4 Knead lightly, roll out as required.

Pancakes

cooking time about 6 minutes each

you will need:

batter:	cooking fat
2 oz. plain flour	lemon
pinch salt	castor sugar
½ egg	
¼ pint milk	

1 Sieve the flour and salt into a mixing bowl. Make a well in the centre and add the half egg.
2 Add about half the milk and stir, gradually working in the flour from the sides.
3 Add enough milk to give a stiff batter consistency. Beat thoroughly for at least 5 minutes, then cover and leave to stand for 30 minutes.
4 Add the remaining milk and stir well. Pour the mixture into a jug.
5 Melt about ½ oz. fat in a small clean frying pan or omelette pan.
6 Just as the fat is beginning to smoke, pour in just enough batter to cover the bottom of the pan thinly. Tilt the pan to ensure the batter runs over evenly.
7 Move the frying pan gently over a quick heat until the pancake is set and brown underneath. Make sure it is loose at the sides and turn it over with a fish slice or a broad bladed knife.
8 Brown on the other side and turn on to a sugared sheet of greaseproof paper. Sprinkle with sugar and lemon juice and roll up. Keep hot while cooking the rest.
9 Serve the pancakes sprinkled with castor sugar and accompanied by wedges of lemon.

Jam pancakes

Make the pancakes as for plain pancakes and spread with jam before rolling up.

Savoury pancakes

Make as above. Fill as for omelettes (see pages 34, 35).

Potato dumplings

cooking time 35 minutes

you will need:

8 oz. potatoes	2½ oz. plain flour
¼ level teaspoon salt	

1 Peel potatoes and boil in salted water.
2 Drain and mash well, or, rub through a sieve.
3 Add salt and flour and knead to a smooth dough.
4 Divide into 2 pieces and roll each to a sausage about ¾ inch thick.
5 Cut in ¾-inch pieces, dip in flour and form into small balls.
6 Drop in fast boiling salted water, or soup.
7 Boil rapidly for 10 minutes. Drain and serve hot.
8 They can be added to stew as for dumplings, or served separately with tomato sauce (see page 69) and grated cheese.

French batter

you will need:

2 oz. flour	pinch salt
1 egg separated	⅛ pint tepid water
1 dessertspoon oil	

1 Sift flour and salt together.
2 Make a well in the centre and add the oil and the egg yolk.
3 Gradually add the water, mixing to a smooth batter.
4 Leave to stand for at least 1 hour.
5 Just before using, fold in the stiffly whisked egg white.
6 Use for coating fruit fritters, onions, chicken or scampi.

White sauce

cooking time about 10 minutes

you will need:

1 oz. butter	½ pint milk
1 oz. flour	seasoning

1 Melt the butter, stir in the flour using a wooden spoon.
2 Cook over a gentle heat for 3 minutes without browning, stirring all the time.
3 Remove from the heat and gradually stir in half the milk, stir hard until well blended.
4 Return to the heat and cook slowly until sauce thickens, stirring.
5 Gradually add remaining liquid.
6 Bring to the boil, season with salt and pepper. Allow to boil for 2–3 minutes, stirring throughout.

Note:

This is a thick or coating surface, used for cauliflower cheese, filling flans and baked casserole dishes. For a thin or pouring sauce, use ½ oz. butter and ½ oz. flour. The amount of milk and the method is the same.

Cheese sauce

To ½ pint white sauce add 2 heaped table-spoons grated cheese, a little made mustard, a little salt and a pinch of cayenne pepper. Add the cheese when the sauce is at boiling point, mix well in but do not allow the sauce to boil again.

Mushroom sauce

Cook 2 oz. sliced mushrooms in ½ oz. butter very gently for about 15 minutes. Stir the mushrooms, butter and the juice into ½ pint hot white sauce. Season to taste.

Onion sauce

To ½ pint white sauce (made from half milk and half liquid in which the onions were cooked) add 2 chopped, boiled onions and a few drops of lemon juice.

Parsley sauce

To ½ pint boiling white sauce, add 1 heaped tablespoon chopped parsley and a squeeze of lemon juice, if liked.

Egg sauce

Stir 1 or 2 chopped hard-boiled eggs into ½ pint white sauce, after it has boiled.

Sweet sauce

Omit seasoning, stir 1 oz. sugar and 2–3 drops flavouring essence into half pint hot white sauce. Stir until sugar is dissolved.

Creamy cheese sauce

cooking time 5 minutes

you will need:

½ small can evaporated milk   ¼ teaspoon dry mustard
pinch salt   1 teaspoon Worcester-
2–3 oz. processed cheese,   shire sauce
   chopped or shredded

1 Put the milk, salt and cheese into a bowl over a pan of hot water.
2 Heat gently stirring all the time until the cheese melts.
3 Add the mustard and Worcestershire sauce.
4 Cook 2–3 minutes longer until sauce thickens.
5 Serve hot, poured over fish or vegetables. This sauce can be used cold, spread on toast and grilled.

Tomato sauce

cooking time about 30 minutes

you will need:

1 onion   pinch thyme
1 tablespoon oil   ½ pint water
½ small can tomato purée   salt and pepper

1 Peel and chop the onion.
2 Heat the oil in a small pan and fry the onion for about 5 minutes.
3 Add the tomato purée and cook for a few minutes longer.
4 Stir all the time.
5 Add the thyme and water, boil gently for about 25 minutes.
6 Season to taste.

Hollandaise sauce

cooking time 5–8 minutes

you will need:

2 tablespoons wine vinegar   salt and pepper
2 egg yolks   lemon juice
2–4 oz. butter

1 Boil the vinegar in a small pan until it has reduced by half. Allow to become cool.
2 Mix the egg yolks and vinegar together in a basin and place over hot water. Whisk until beginning to thicken, then very gradually whisk in the butter until all is absorbed.
3 Season and add lemon juice to taste.
4 Serve immediately with fish or broccoli.

Sour cream sauce

cooking time 10–15 minutes

you will need:

¼ pint sour cream	¼ pint milk or stock
2 tablespoons butter	salt and pepper
1 tablespoon flour	

1 Melt the butter, stir in the flour and cook over a gentle heat for 3 minutes.
2 Gradually stir in the milk or stock and bring to the boil, reduce the heat and simmer for 5–10 minutes.
3 Stir in the sour cream and season.
4 Serve with liver, vegetables or fish.

Note:

If soured or cultured cream is not available, stir 1 dessertspoon lemon juice into ¼ pint real dairy cream and leave in a warm place for 10 minutes.

Curry sauce

cooking time 40 minutes

you will need:

1 onion	½ oz. curry powder
1 small apple	1 teaspoon curry paste
1 oz. fat	(optional)
1 oz. flour	½ pint stock
1 oz. sultanas	

1 Peel and chop onion and apple.
2 Melt fat, fry onion and apple until brown.
3 Blend in flour, curry powder and paste if used and cook for 3 minutes.
4 Gradually stir in liquid.
5 Bring to the boil, stirring.
6 Reduce heat, add sultanas, cover and simmer for at least 30 minutes.

Horseradish cream

you will need:

2 tablespoons grated horseradish	salt and pepper to taste mixed mustard to taste
1 tablespoon wine vinegar or lemon juice	¼ pint cream
2 teaspoons castor sugar	

1 Mix all the ingredients together in a bowl, except the cream.
2 Whisk the cream lightly until a trail from the whisk just shows on the surface.
3 Gently fold the horseradish mixture into the cream. Serve very cold (if liked, chill and serve semi-solid). Serve with beef or ham.

Sweet sauce

(suitable for serving with steamed or baked puddings)

cooking time about 10 minutes

you will need:

1 tablespoon jam or marmalade	½ level teaspoon cornflour few drops lemon juice
¼ pint water	(optional)

1 Blend the cornflour with a little of the water.
2 Bring the remainder of the water to the boil, pour on to the cornflour, stirring all the time.
3 Rinse the pan with cold water, pour the sauce back and bring to the boil. Add jam. Boil for 3 minutes, add lemon juice to taste if liked.

Chocolate sauce

cooking time about 10 minutes

you will need:

2 oz. plain chocolate	½ small can evaporated
2 oz. castor sugar	milk

1 Grate chocolate into a basin, place over a pan of hot water.
2 Heat until chocolate is melted.
3 Add sugar and milk and stir over heat until sugar dissolves.
4 Use at once or leave over gentle heat until required.

Use hot chocolate sauce poured over ice cream, bananas, canned pears or a slice of lemon mousse.

French dressing

you will need:

¼ teaspoon salt	2 teaspoons malt, tarragon
shake pepper	or wine vinegar
1½ tablespoons olive oil	

1 Mix the salt and pepper with the oil, then add the vinegar and mix till well emulsified.
2 A little dry mustard, crushed garlic or chopped herbs may be added as liked, these are added to the oil before the vinegar is added.

Mayonnaise

you will need:

1 egg yolk	2 teaspoons vinegar
¼ teaspoon made mustard	(white and tarragon)
pepper and salt	or lemon juice and
3–4 tablespoons olive oil	tarragon vinegar

Mix the egg yolk, mustard, pepper and salt.
Add the oil drop by drop, either stirring with
a wooden spoon or whisking until the sauce
is thick and smooth.
Add the vinegar gradually and mix thoroughly.

Cream salad dressing

you will need:

1 saltspoon made mustard	2 tablespoons double
1 saltspoon salt	cream
pepper	1 tablespoon oil
pinch castor sugar	1 dessertspoon vinegar (a
	mixture of malt and
	tarragon)

Mix the mustard, salt, pepper to taste and the
castor sugar together. Stir in the cream.
Add the oil, drop by drop, stirring all the time.
Add the vinegar slowly and stir well.

Sour cream dressing

you will need:

thick sour cream	little made mustard
seasoning	little castor sugar

Place the cream in a bowl and stir until
smooth.
Season to taste with salt, pepper, mustard and
sugar.
If the dressing is very thick, it can be thinned
down with a little top of the milk.

Cooked salad dressing

cooking time about 15 minutes

you will need:

¼ pint fairly thick white	1 tablespoon malt vinegar
sauce (see page 68)	½ tablespoon tarragon
1 egg yolk	vinegar
salt and pepper	

1 Make the sauce and remove from the heat.
Stir in the beaten egg yolk and season to taste.
2 Cook very gently over a low heat. Do not boil.
3 Stir in the vinegars and use as required. The
dressing will keep for a short time, stored in a
cool place.

Maître d'hôtel butter

you will need:

1 oz. fresh butter	few drops lemon juice
1 teaspoon parsley, finely	
chopped	

1 Cream butter with a wooden spoon until soft.
2 Beat in parsley and lemon juice to taste.
3 Form into a 'pat' and leave in a cold place
until firm.
4 Serve on grilled fish or meat.

Veal forcemeat

you will need:

4 oz. breadcrumbs	½ teaspoon chopped mixed
2 oz. chopped suet or	herbs
margarine	nutmeg
1 tablespoon chopped	grated rind ½ lemon
parsley	salt and pepper
1 beaten egg	

1 Mix all the ingredients together, seasoning to
taste.

Sage and onion stuffing

cooking time 10 minutes

you will need:

2 oz. onions	1 oz. butter
4 sage leaves or ½ teaspoon	salt and pepper
powdered sage	½ egg (optional)
2 oz. breadcrumbs	

1 Slice the onions thickly and parboil for 10
minutes in a very little water.
2 Scald the sage leaves.
3 Chop the onions and sage leaves.
4 Mash and work all the ingredients together.
Season to taste.

To boil rice

1 Use plenty of water and if the rice is required for savoury dishes add salt to the water. Use $1\frac{1}{2}$-2 pints of water and 1 teaspoon of salt to each 2 oz. rice.
2 When the water boils, add the washed rice and keep rapidly boiling. Do not put the lid on the pan.
3 Boil until just tender. The time varies from 5 to 15 minutes according to the type of rice.

Do not overcook. To test if the rice is cooked squeeze a grain between the thumb and first finger. If it is not cooked there will be a hard particle of starch in the centre of each grain. When cooked it will be quite soft.
4 Turn into a colander or sieve and pour boiling water through it to remove any loose starch and to separate the grains. Cover with a cloth and leave to dry for a few minutes in a warm place or put on a tray covered with grease-proof paper in a cool oven.

Ideas for Left-Overs

Even if you buy the small size of canned fruit or vegetables you may find that there is some left over. Not enough for a full serving—but don't throw it away. There are many ways of using these bits to add flavour or variety to well-known dishes.

22 ideas for using up canned fruit

1 Fry 2 or 3 apricots or a pineapple ring with bacon.

2 Add apricots tossed in mayonnaise or French dressing to a salad.

3 Chop apricots, use as a pancake filling, boil syrup from the fruit and serve as a hot sauce with the pancake.

4 Use chopped apricots mixed with raisins as a tart filling.

5 Top baked milk pudding with apricots, sprinkle with coconut.

6 Mix cherries with cream cheese, use as the main ingredient in a salad.

7 Spoon cherries with juice over a banana, heat through, serve as a sweet.

8 Try a few sliced peaches on buttered brown bread or scones instead of jam.

9 Toss a halved peach in desiccated coconut, top with ice cream.

10 Fill a peach half with raspberry jam or mincemeat, serve with thin custard or cream.

11 Add a peach half, sprinkled with chopped nuts, to a ham or cheese salad.

12 Add a few sliced peaches to apple pie for an unusual flavour.

13 Serve a canned pear, sprinkled with French dressing and filled with cottage cheese on lettuce for a quick salad.

14 Sprinkle a pear half with grated cheese, grill and serve with cold ham for a change.

15 Heat a pear half in its own syrup, flavour with cinnamon, serve hot with cream.

16 Melt two squares of chocolate, spoon on to a halved pear for a quick sweet.

17 Pile chopped nuts and dates on to a pear half, sprinkle with grated cheese. Serve with mayonnaise for a nutritious salad.

18 Add drained crushed pineapple to a bread pudding in place of dried fruit.

19 Crushed pineapple blended with butter or cream cheese is delicious on toast or as a sandwich filling.

20 Try a spoonful of crushed pineapple with cold meat instead of chutney.

Heat 2 or 3 plums in their own syrup, serve hot on vanilla ice cream.

Spread wholemeal biscuits with cream cheese, top with a chopped plum for a teatime treat.

14 ideas for using up canned vegetables

Add carrots or peas to hot thin white sauce, heat through, sprinkle with grated nutmeg for an unusual vegetable.

When heating canned peas—add a thin slice of onion.

When reheating peas—fry a rasher of bacon in the pan first.

Cooked peas mixed with mayonnaise make a good addition to a salad especially with ham or hard-boiled egg.

Chopped cooked spinach makes a tasty filling for a baked potato or onion. Sprinkle with grated cheese before serving.

Spread cooked spinach on a slice of ham, roll up and heat through in cheese sauce for a simple meal.

Put a layer of spinach in the bottom of the dish before cooking macaroni cheese.

Heat green beans in melted butter, sprinkle with grated nutmeg for a change.

Heat left-over canned tomatoes, add green beans for an unusual vegetable.

Sprinkle green beans with finely chopped onion and French dressing, add to a salad.

Hot canned tomatoes with a pinch of sugar added make a delicious sauce for fish or chops.

Mix canned tomatoes with cooked cauliflower, sprinkle with grated cheese and breadcrumbs, brown under the grill.

Fry a sliced onion in butter, add left-over tomatoes. Heat through as an extra vegetable.

Heat canned tomatoes, pour over a hard-boiled egg, halved lengthways, for a tasty snack. Add boiled rice or sweet corn to make a meal.

Quick snacks from left-overs

1 Grill 2–4 rashers bacon. Place in the bottom of the grill pan under the rack. Grill 1–2 pineapple rings until brown on one side. Turn over, top with a slice of cheese and continue to grill until the cheese melts and becomes brown. Top with the bacon and serve.

2 Mix together cold, cooked Patna rice, chopped skinned tomato, chopped cooked ham. Add 1–2 slices stuffed olives (optional) and moisten with well seasoned French dressing.

3 Melt a little fat in a frying pan and sauté cold cooked chopped potatoes until brown. Push to one side of the pan and add 2–3 rashers bacon with rinds removed. When cooked, push to one side of the pan with the potato. Add one egg to the pan and fry until cooked. Turn the potatoes on to a hot plate, top with the bacon and place the fried egg on top of the bacon. Serve with watercress.

4 Mix together cold, chopped, cooked chicken or ham and chopped celery. Bind together with mayonnaise to which a little made mustard has been added. Serve with watercress and crispbreads or brown bread and butter.

5 Melt enough butter to cover the bottom of a small saucepan. Add any cold flaked fish and a pinch of mixed herbs. Heat through very gently. Add about 1 teaspoon lemon juice and, if liked, a little cream. Serve on toasted brown bread.

6 Slice cold cooked sausages very thinly and mix lightly with mango chutney. Serve with French bread and watercress.

7 Finely grate 1 small apple and 1 carrot. Mix with a little chopped chicory and chopped hard-boiled egg. Moisten lightly with French dressing.

8 Chop a few slices of liver sausage and add to coleslaw. Serve with potato crisps and lettuce.

9 Peel and quarter a small orange and cut each segment in half. Mix with the flesh from half a grapefruit, pile into the grapefruit shell, sprinkle with castor sugar and leave for about 30 minutes. Serve with sponge finger biscuits, as a sweet.

10 For a quick refreshing sweet, chop 1 small apple (do not remove the peel) and 1 small pear. Mix with 1 carton of natural yoghourt and leave in a cool place for about 30 minutes. If preferred, slice 1 banana, add to a carton of yoghourt and serve sprinkled with brown sugar.

11 Stir blackcurrant jam to taste into apple purée and serve with cream and sponge finger biscuits.
12 Milk or plain jellies can be 'finished-up' in the following ways:
Sprinkled with grated chocolate or desiccated coconut;
Topped with a few chopped nuts and glacé cherries;
Orange jelly topped with segments of fresh orange;
Lemon jelly sprinkled with finely crushed ginger biscuits, or sprinkled with crushed chocolate digestive biscuits.

Meal planning

Young people living alone for the first time are often tempted to 'skimp' meals or miss them out completely either because they find that the 'housekeeping' money just will not go round, that it is too difficult to cook in a bedsitter or that they are too busy enjoying their independence. Baked beans on toast is not an adequate meal if you have been busy all day and have not had a good midday meal. Good looks and vitality will never be yours if you are not sensible about your meals. Base your food for the day on two really good meals, and make these breakfast and dinner, either at midday or in the evening.

A good breakfast is very important, for after seven or eight hours without anything to eat you need something which will keep you going for another four or five hours. With a good breakfast you will not be so inclined to have biscuits or a buttered bun with your coffee. If you do not like to eat a hot cooked breakfast try cold boiled bacon for a change. A small joint cooked and cut into slices is very tasty and nourishing and could be eaten with a poached egg, or a tomato, or a canned pineapple ring. Slices of Cheddar cheese with fresh fruit and toast, yoghourt and fruit, or muesli (see page 45) all make a good start to the day.

If you are not able to have a cooked meal at lunch time, you must be firm with yourself and take a good meal with you. A packed meal can be nutritious and interesting and it is well worth while putting yourself to the trouble of being well organised so that your 'meal at the desk' is worth eating.

If you take sandwiches see that you include an ingredient which will provide protein (meat, eggs, cheese, fish), some fresh fruit or a tomato, better still both. And if you are watching your waistline don't forget that starch reduced breads, crispbreads and rolls can be used in place of other breads. You will find ideas for making sandwiches on the following pages, but do not think that a packed meal need only be restricted to sandwiches. With the advantages of aluminium foil, plastic bags and containers it is no problem to take a salad, it need not be elaborate but think how much good a stuffed hard-boiled egg or ham with lettuce, tomato and watercress followed by an orange will do in providing good looks and vitality compared with a sugary bun and a cup of tea, with possibly a bar of chocolate added to dispel the pangs of hunger which are sure to come later in the day. It is worth investing in a thermos to take soup for a change; a vegetable soup and a chunk of cheese and an apple make a good lunch and is no problem to eat at your place of work. If you are eating in your office most days it is important to keep the necessary 'tools' handy; a knife, fork and plate can be popped into a plastic bag and kept in a drawer, salt and pepper are essential and it is worth buying a cheap container for these, rather than risking having them spill all over the office. A supply of tissues is always useful too.

Hints on making sandwiches

1 Ring the changes by using different breads; choose from farmhouse, Vienna, bloomer, brown wheat germ, wholemeal, rye, malt and currant. Try using two different breads in the same sandwich, for example, white and wholemeal or white and malt, currant and milk bread.
2 The bread should be thinly cut, and you will find that it is easier to cut if it is a day old. If you have a refrigerator store the bread for a few hours before cutting if you think that it is going to be difficult.

If you like to take rolls for a change, these must be new and crisp. Choose one of the following varieties: bap, bridge, baton or dinner rolls.

Butter will spread more easily if you beat in a little hot water—a dessertspoon to 4 oz. butter will make a creamy spread that will not harden.

Spread the butter evenly all over the bread, right up to the crusts; this will help to water-proof the bread.

If you make up sandwiches the night before they are required, do not add sliced tomatoes, cucumber, beetroot or lettuce. These will make the bread soggy; they should be taken separately and 'tucked into' the sandwich at the last minute.

Sandwiches will keep moist and fresh wrapped in aluminium foil, polythene bags or in grease-proof paper then in a damp cloth.

If the sandwich filling is dry, as with sliced meat or ham or cheese, moisten with a little mayonnaise, pickles or chutney.

If you are taking sandwiches with different fillings, wrap each separately so that the flavours retain their individuality.

Keep sandwiches in a cool place until required.

Sandwiches to make a meal

Thinly sliced roast lamb with slices of unpeeled cucumber moistened with mint sauce, or mayonnaise sprinkled with a little chopped mint or parsley

Slices of cold boiled bacon or ham with thin slices of Cheddar cheese and apple sauce

Slices of roast beef with thin slices of tomato and thinly sliced raw onion

Cream cheese with chopped cooked dried apricots and roughly chopped walnuts

Cottage cheese with chopped cooked rashers of bacon and grated eating apple or chopped canned pineapple

Mixed chopped chicken and celery moistened with mayonnaise and chopped toasted almonds

Chopped hard-boiled egg and anchovy fillets moistened with mayonnaise

Peanut butter, sliced apple sprinkled with lemon juice and crisp fried bacon rashers

Sliced liver sausage, hard-boiled egg and sweet pickle or chutney

Grated Cheddar cheese mixed with grated carrot and mayonnaise

Flaked corned beef mixed with grated cheese with a little horseradish sauce

Chopped tongue mixed with chopped hard-boiled egg, mixed with mayonnaise flavoured with a little curry powder

Slices of cooked brisket of beef with finely shredded cabbage bound with mayonnaise or cultured cream

Mashed sardines mixed with grated cheese, flavoured with lemon juice

Sandwiches for the sweet course

Grated apple tossed in lemon juice, mixed with thick honey and raisins.

Full fruit apricot jam sprinkled with desiccated coconut

Mashed banana sprinkled with lemon juice and mixed with finely chopped dates

Cherry jam or currant jelly and cottage or cream cheese

Grated eating apple tossed in lemon juice mixed with roughly grated chocolate.

Cream or cottage cheese mixed with drained canned peaches, chopped

Finger food for the lunch box

Cooked sausages cut through and sandwiched with tomato sauce or chutney

Grated Cheddar cheese mixed with a little milk or mayonnaise, formed into balls and rolled in chopped nuts

Sections of eating apple or drained canned pineapple wrapped in slices of cooked ham

Pieces of celery filled with cream or cottage cheese

Slices of cooked beef spread with cream cheese flavoured with curry powder and rolled up

Hard-boiled eggs, cut in half, yolk mixed with sandwich spread or sweet pickle, stuffed back into the white and the two halves sandwiched together again

Cold cooked hamburger, cut in half and spread lightly with mustard or sauce.

Eating apple, core removed, stuffed with grated cheese mixed with raisins or with cooked chopped meat bound with mayonnaise

Fish fingers fried in butter and allowed to become cold

Slices of pork luncheon meat sandwiched together with thin slices of cheese spread with chutney

Large firm tomato stuffed with mixed vegetable salad, or cold scrambled egg

Left-over bread

Living alone you will probably find that you often have bread to use up. It is surprising how long one small loaf lasts if there is only one person to eat it. If you are prepared to spend a little time you will find that it can be used up in a variety of useful ways. If you prefer to eat the starch reduced protein enriched breads you will find that they make particularly fine light 'raspings' which can be used for coating food before frying or for giving a crunchy topping to meat, fish, eggs or vegetables which are served in a sauce.

To make raspings

Place all the pieces of bread, crusts and really stale ends included, in a baking tin and leave in a slow oven for several hours until crisp and pale golden in colour. When cold spread out between two sheets of foil or greaseproof paper and crush with a rolling pin. Shake through a sieve, if available, and store the fine crumbs in a covered jar.

Another handy way of using up pieces of bread is to make buttered breadcrumbs. These can be stored in a covered jar in a cold place for at least a month.

To make buttered breadcrumbs

Grate 4 oz. dry white bread. Melt 2 oz. butter, add the crumbs and cook over a very gentle heat, stirring with a fork. Continue cooking until the crumbs are deep gold in colour and crisp. They may be used at once or if to be stored for any length of time, spread the crumbs out on a baking tray and dry out in a cool oven.

To use, sprinkle over cheese or fish dishes, or over cooked vegetables. The crumbs may be reheated gently before use. Sweet buttered crumbs can be made by preparing the crumbs as above, with 1 oz. castor sugar added to the mixture in the pan. Finely grated orange or lemon rind may be added to the cold crumbs before they are stored. Use the sweet crumbs sprinkled on stewed fruit, milk puddings or ice-cream. A small pinch of mixed spice or cinnamon may be added to the crumbs if liked. For a quick sweet, mix crumbs with sultanas and sliced banana, serve with thin custard or cream. Or arrange crumbs in layers with canned or stewed fruit in a pie dish and bake in a moderate oven for about 30 minutes. Serve hot or cold.

And here are a few more ways of using up bread; you will want to try these whether the bread is really left over or not.

Continental rusks

Spread thick slices of bread with butter on each side, place on a baking tray and bake in a slow oven for 1 hour. Use hot or cold as an accompaniment to soup or in the Continental style with chocolate or coffee.

Cheese rusks

These can be prepared by sprinkling the buttered bread with grated cheese and baked as for Continental rusks. A sprinkle of grated nutmeg, paprika or garlic salt may be added if liked.

Sugared rusks

Cream an equal quantity of butter and sugar, adding a little hot milk and a pinch of cinnamon if liked. Spread on each side of thick slices of bread and bake in a slow oven for 1 hour. These rusks make a delicious accompaniment to stewed fruit, fruit fool or baked custard. They can be served at breakfast too, with cooked dried apricots or prunes.

Split toast

Cut bread in slices $\frac{1}{2}$ inch thick. Toast on both sides. Split through with a sharp knife. Toast the uncooked side under a low grill until crisp and dry.

Melba toast

Cut very thin slices of bread, removing the crust.

Spread on a baking tray and bake in a slow oven for about 1 hour.

Both these 'toasts' can be stored in an airtight tin when completely cold. Serve as an accompaniment to soup, with pâté or savoury paste or cheese spread. If the melba toast is required for 'dipping' cut it into fingers before baking.

Equivalent measures

Ingredients	Measure	Weight	Measure	Weight
Breadcrumbs	1 cup	2½ oz.	3½ tablespoons	1 oz.
Butter and other fats	1 cup	6 oz.	1 level tablespoon	1 oz.
Candied peel chopped	1 cup	4½ oz.	1 tablespoon	½ oz.
Castor sugar	1 cup	7½ oz.	1 level tablespoon	1 oz.
Cornflour	1 cup	4 oz.	2 level tablespoons	1 oz.
Currants	1 cup	6 oz.	1 tablespoon	1 oz.
Curry powder			2 heaped tablespoons	1 oz.
Egg, medium, new laid	1	2 oz.		
Fish, flaked, cooked	1 cup	6 oz.	1 level tablespoon	1 oz.
Flour	1 cup	4 oz.	1 rounded tablespoon	1 oz.
Granulated sugar	1 cup	7½ oz.	1 tablespoon	1 oz.
Grated cheese	1 cup	2½ oz.	2 heaped tablespoons	1 oz.
Ground coffee	1 cup	2 oz.	2 heaped tablespoons	1 oz.
Jam	1 cup	8 oz.	1 rounded tablespoon	1 oz.
Loaf sugar	1 cup	4½ oz.	7 lumps	1 oz.
Meat, cooked, diced	1 cup	4 oz.		
Meat, cooked, minced	1 cup	5 oz.		
Oatmeal	1 cup	4 oz.	1 rounded tablespoon	1 oz.
Peas, dried	1 cup	8 oz.	1 level tablespoon	1 oz.
Rice	1 cup	6 oz.	1 tablespoon	1 oz.
Suet, shredded	1 cup	4½ oz.	1 tablespoon	1 oz.
Sultanas	1 cup	4 oz.	1 rounded tablespoon	1 oz.
Syrup	1 cup	8 oz.	1 dessert spoon	1 oz.
Vegetables, root chopped or diced	1 cup	5 oz.		

8 tablespoons are equivalent to ¼ pint of liquid.

Calorie Values

Food	Amount	Calories
BEVERAGES		
Beer—ale, mild	½ pint	130
Beer—ale, pale	½ pint	150
Beer—ale, strong	½ pint	210
Beer—stout	½ pint	140
Cider	½ pint	120
Chocolate	1 cup	180
Cocoa (half milk)	1 cup	110
Coffee—black	1 cup	0
Coffee—milk, no sugar	1 cup	30
Coffee—milk and sugar	1 cup	85
Fruit juice, diluted	1 glass	100
Malted drinks	1 cup	205
Mineral waters (artificial)	1 glass	100
Spirits (brandy, gin, rum, whisky)	1 oz.	75
Tea—milk, no sugar	1 cup	20
Tea—milk and sugar	1 cup	75
Wines—port	2 oz.	90
Wines—sherry	2 oz.	90
Wines, table—dry	4 oz.	70
Wines, table—sweet	4 oz.	90
BISCUITS		
Biscuits—plain	1 oz.	105—115
Biscuits—sweet	1 oz.	135—145
Starch reduced crispbread	1 oz.	110—120
BREAD		
Bread—wholemeal, brown or white fresh or toasted	1 oz.	70
Starch reduced roll	1 roll	18

Food	Amount	Calories
CAKES		
Cake—plain	1 slice (2 oz.)	150
Cake—rich, iced	1 slice (2 oz.)	210
Doughnut	2 oz.	195
Fruit cake	1 slice (2 oz.)	180
CEREALS		
Arrowroot	1 oz.	100
Barley—pearl, dry	1 oz.	95
Cornflour—custard powder	1 oz.	100
Cornflakes and other breakfast cereals	1 oz.	106—110
Flour	1 oz.	100
Lentils—dried	1 oz.	164
Macaroni—uncooked	1 oz.	80—100
Maize meal—raw	1 oz.	95
Oatmeal	1 oz.	110
Rice—dry	1 oz.	90
Sago—dry	2 oz.	195
Soya flour (whole)	1 oz.	120
Soya flour, low fat	1 oz.	95
Spaghetti—dry	1 oz.	80
Tapioca—dry	2 oz.	195
CHEESE		
Cheese—Cheddar	1 oz.	120
Cheese—cottage	1 oz.	40—50
Cheese—cream	1 oz.	145
Cheese—Dutch	1 oz.	90
Processed	1 oz.	120

Calorie Values

Food	Amount	Calories
EGGS		
Eggs—raw	1 (2 oz.)	80
Eggs—boiled	1	80
Eggs—poached	1	80—120
		(if cooked in poacher with butter)
Eggs—fried	1	120—140
		(depending on amount of fat)
Eggs—scrambled	1	ditto
Egg white	1	11
Egg yolk	1	69
FATS AND MILK		
Butter	$\frac{1}{4}$ oz.	65
Lard	$\frac{1}{4}$ oz.	60
Margarine	$\frac{1}{4}$ oz.	55
Milk—whole	$\frac{1}{2}$ pint	166—180
Milk—skimmed	$\frac{1}{2}$ pint	70
Milk—condensed	1 oz.	100
Milk—evaporated	1 oz.	45
Cream—light	1 oz.	55
Cream—heavy	1 oz.	100
Yoghourt	$\frac{1}{4}$ pint	100
FISH		
Crab	2 oz.	75
Cod Fillets	4 oz.	95
Haddock—fresh	4 oz.	115
Haddock—smoked	4 oz.	120
Halibut	4 oz.	140
Hake	4 oz.	90
Herring (1)	4 oz.	190
Lobster	4 oz.	65
Mackerel	4 oz.	90

Food	Amount	Calories
FISH—cont.		
Oysters	6 medium	65
Plaice	4 oz.	90
Salmon—fresh	4 oz.	155
Salmon—canned	4 oz.	190
Salmon—smoked	2 oz.	175
Sardines	2 oz.	160
Shrimps	4 oz.	55
Sole	4 oz.	90
Sprats	4 oz.	170
		(if cooked without fat)
FRUIT		
Apple—cooked	5 oz.	75
Apple (1)	approx. 4 oz.	45
Apricots—fresh	approx. 4 oz.	30
Apricots—canned	4 oz.	60
Apricots—dried	1 oz.	50
Banana (1 average)		80—100
Blackberries—fresh	2 oz.	15
Blackberries—canned	4 oz.	75
Cherries—fresh	4 oz.	45
Cherries—canned	4 oz.	95
Coconut—fresh	1 oz.	170
Coconut—desiccated	1 oz.	180
Dates—dried	1 oz.	85
Figs—dried	1 oz.	115
Gooseberries	4 oz.	40
Grapefruit	4 oz.	25
Grapes	4 oz.	60
Lemon (1)	3 oz.	30
Loganberries	4 oz.	20
Melon	1 oz.	4
Olives	$\frac{1}{2}$ oz.	25

Calorie Values

Food	Amount	Calories	Food	Amount	Calories
FRUIT—cont.			MEAT—cont.		
Orange (1)	6 oz.	40	Steak	4 oz.	300
Peaches—fresh	4 oz.	30	Tongue	4 oz.	290
Peaches—canned	4 oz.	64	Veal and ham pie	4 oz.	300
Pear—fresh	6 oz.	50	Veal—lean	4 oz.	145
Pear—canned	2 halves	75	Sweetbreads	4 oz.	250
Pineapple—fresh	6 oz.	65			
Pineapple—canned	6 oz.	120	MISCELLANEOUS		
Plums—fresh	4 oz.	30	Cocoa powder	$\frac{1}{4}$ oz.	30
Plums—canned	4 oz.	80	Gelatine	$\frac{1}{4}$ oz.	25
Prunes—dried	2 oz.	75	Honey	1 oz.	80
Raisins	2 oz.	125	Ice cream (vanilla)	2 oz.	115
Raspberries—fresh	4 oz.	25	Jams and jellies	$\frac{1}{2}$ oz.	35—60
Rhubarb	4 oz.	5	Jelly—dessert	4 oz.	85—100
Strawberries	4 oz.	30	Junket	$\frac{1}{2}$ pint	166—180
Tangerines	2 small	40	Marmalade	$\frac{1}{2}$ oz.	35
			Oils—salad	$\frac{1}{4}$ ounce	60
MEAT			Pickles		
Bacon—lean	2 oz.	175	(non-thickened)	1 spoon	5—10
Bacon—fat	2 oz.	260	Soup—thin	4 oz.	20
Beef—corned	4 oz.	280	Soup—creamy	5 oz.	80
Beef—roast lean	4 oz.	210			upwards
Beef—roast with fat	4 oz.	up to 300			
Ham—lean	4 oz.	265	NUTS		
Ham—fat	4 oz.	375	Almonds	1 oz.	170
Heart	4 oz.	265	Brazil nuts	1 oz.	90
Kidneys	4 oz.	145	Chestnuts	2 oz.	75
Lamb—lean	4 oz.	230	Peanuts	2 oz.	335
Lamb—fat	4 oz.	375	Walnuts	1 oz.	185
Liver	4 oz.	160			
Mutton—lean	4 oz.	230			
Mutton—fat	4 oz.	370	POULTRY		
Pork—lean	4 oz.	270	Chicken	4 oz.	165
Pork—fat	4 oz.	450	Duck	4 oz.	190
Sausages—beef	2 oz.	145	Goose	4 oz.	355
Sausages—pork	2 oz.	145	Turkey	4 oz.	185

Calorie Values

Food	Amount	Calories	Food	Amount	Calories
SUGAR AND SWEETS			**VEGETABLES—cont.**		
Sugar—white	$\frac{1}{2}$ oz.	55	Carrots	2 oz.	15
Sugar—brown	$\frac{1}{2}$ oz.	50	Cauliflower	4 oz.	20
Syrup	1 oz.	80	Celery	2 oz.	5
Boiled sweets	1 oz.	120 approx.	Cucumber	2 oz.	10
			Endive	2 oz.	5
Chocolate—plain	1 oz.	150	Leeks	4 oz.	15
Chocolate—milk	1 oz.	150	Lettuce	2 oz.	10
			Marrow	4 oz.	10
			Mushrooms	2 oz.	2
			Onions	4 oz.	25
VEGETABLES			Parsley	$\frac{1}{4}$ oz.	0
Asparagus	6 stalks (3 oz.)	15	Parsnips	4 oz.	55
			Peas—canned	4 oz.	25
Beans—baked	4 oz.	100	Peas—fresh	4 oz.	75
Beans—broad	1 oz.	15	Peas—dried	1 oz.	85
Beans—butter, boiled	1 oz.	25	Pepper (vegetable)	1 oz.	10
Beans—haricot, dried	1 oz.	70	Potatoes (boiled)	2 medium (4 oz.)	95
Beans—French or runner	4 oz.	15	Potatoes—fried	4 oz.	270
Beetroot	2 oz.	15	Radishes	1 oz.	2
Broccoli	4 oz.	15	Spinach	4 oz.	20
Brussels sprouts	4 oz.	20	Tomatoes—fresh	4 oz.	20
Cabbage	4 oz.	20	Tomatoes—juice	4 oz.	25
			Turnips	4 oz.	40

Basic Methods of Cooking

Baking
Cooking in dry heat in the oven.

Boiling
Cooking by immersing the food in a pan of liquid, which must be kept boiling gently—all the time.

Braising
Almost a combination of stewing and roasting. Meat is placed on a bed of vegetables with a little liquid surrounding, in a covered vessel, and cooked slowly in the oven.

Casserole
Cooking slowly in the oven in a covered casserole dish—usually meat, rabbit, etc.

Frying
Cooking in a little hot fat in an open pan. Deep frying is cooking by immersion in a deep pan of smoking hot fat.

Grilling
Cooking quickly under a red-hot grill: used for small tender pieces of meat, fish, etc.

Poaching
Cooking gently in water which is just below boiling point: usually eggs or fish.

Pressure Cooking
Cooking at higher temperatures than usual, so that food is cooked much more quickly.

Roasting
Cooking with a little fat in a hot oven. Fat is poured from the baking tin over the meat or poultry from time to time, using a long-handled spoon: this is known as basting.

Simmering
The rate of cooking used for stews—just below boiling point, so that the liquid bubbles gently at the side of the pan.

Steaming
Cooking either in a steamer over a pan of boiling water, or in a basin standing in (but not covered by) boiling water.

Stewing
Cooking slowly until the food is tender. It is done in just enough liquid to cover the food, as the liquid is served with it and should be rich. Stews may be cooked in covered saucepans or casseroles, on a hotplate or in the oven—but always at a low temperature.

Index

A

Almond:
    Almond cherry dessert, 64
    Almond dessert mould, 44
    Almond flapjacks, 50
    Almond shortbread triangles, 53
    Almond twists, 53
    Apricot almond slices, 54
American beef hash, 28

Apple:
    Apple basket salad, 39
    Apple crumble, 46
    Apple delight, 43, 45
    Apple meringue, 47
    Apple snowball, 43
    Baked apple, 47
    Baked apple, Fillings for, 47
    Cabbage and apple salad, 39

Apricot:
    Apricot almond slices, 54
    Apricot rice pudding, 46
    Apricot surprise cakes, 53
Austrian steak, 13

B

Bacon:
    Bacon and banana savoury, 25
    Bacon grill, 31
    Bacon, To shallow fry, 10
    Baked beans and bacon, 23
    Boiled bacon, 18
    Celery and bacon toast, 29
    Grilled bacon and egg, 4
    Grilled chicken with bacon, 20
    Herring and bacon, 18
    Sandwich snack, 30
    Spaghetti with mushrooms and bacon, 24
Baked apple, 47
Baked apple, Fillings for, 47
Baked beans and bacon, 23
Baked beans and bacon, variations, 23
Baked coconut pudding, 47
Baked custard, 42
Baked eggs with potato, 33
Baked eggs, 33
Baked fish, 18
Baked mushrooms, 37
Baked onion, 37

83

W

Z